THE
LITTLE
BOOK
OF
BERKSHIRE

S TUART H YLTON

First published 2014

The History Press
The Mill, Brimscombe Port
Stroud, Gloucestershire, GL5 2QG
www.thehistorypress.co.uk

British Library Cataloguing in Publication Data.
A catalogue record for this book is available from the British Library.

ISBN 978 0 7509 5851 6

Typesetting and origination by The History Press
Printed in Great Britain by TJ International Ltd, Padstow Cornwall

CONTENTS

INTRODUCTION AND ACKNOWLEDGEMENTS

If you are looking for a comprehensive and authoritative history of Berkshire, this is not it. There is a wealth of good books about every aspect of life in the county, and a visit to your local library or bookseller (or, better still, to the comprehensive local history section of Reading Library, where I researched much of this book) will give you the answer to even the most arcane questions about Berkshire. Those of you who know which buttons to press might even risk the Internet!

My brief was more specific. I was asked to produce a book that would be of interest to anyone with links to Berkshire; something that they could dip into, as the mood took them, and where the mainstream history was combined with spicier (or more speculative) fare, such as the area's most famous ghosts and notorious murderers. As a recipient of one of my previous books in this series put it, 'the ideal book to keep in your loo' – but I drew the line at putting 'now wash your hands' at the top of each page. Like the remit for the BBC (albeit in a slightly more modest way), I set out to inform, educate and entertain, though not necessarily in that order of priority.

I owe a great debt to the many diligent researchers who have studied Berkshire before me. Having done my full share of trawling through ancient archives for many of my previous books, I can readily appreciate their dedication. Unfortunately, in a book like this, I do not have the space to acknowledge them all, or it would no longer be a little book. But if my efforts encourage you to explore some aspect of our past further through them, I hope my debt will be in part repaid.

Enjoy this little book.

Stuart Hylton, 2014

1

WHAT IS BERKSHIRE?

This is not as daft a question as it may appear, for what passes for Berkshire in 2014 is very different to what has been called 'Berkshire' for much of our history. Let's try and make our way through that history.

The area this book will talk about is based mainly on the Berkshire that was formed by the county boundary of 1831 (but which existed for several centuries before that) and which carried on with only minor changes until the wholesale review of 1974.

Berkshire does not appear to have existed as a recognisable separate unit in Roman times. It was a rural area with no major towns of its own. The main settlements nearby were Silchester (Calleva Atrebatum) in what is now Hampshire, and Dorchester (in modern Oxfordshire). That is not to say that the area was uninhabited. There were traces of small-scale Roman settlement throughout the length of Berkshire and, before that, traces of Celtic civilisation. It is thought that the whole of pre-Roman Berkshire fell within the territory of a tribe called the Atrebates, whose northern capital was at the same Calleva that the Romans later developed. There is also evidence to suggest that when Verica, the last leader of the Atrebates, was driven from his lands (including Berkshire) he may have gone to Rome and appealed to them for help. This, it is suggested, may have encouraged the Roman invasion in AD 43.

Berkshire as a separate entity probably dates from the 840s, when Sunningum (East Berkshire) was united with Ashdown (taking in the Berkshire Downs and, probably, the Kennet Valley). It came into being after a spot of unpleasantness (lasting about 200 years) between the rival kingdoms of Wessex and Mercia.

The River Thames forms much of the northern boundary of the county (as it had previously divided Wessex and Mercia), with the rivers Cole, Enborne, Blackwater and Kennet providing other parts of the new county's dividing line. Various more or less minor changes took place over the next millennium, ranging from tidying up parish

boundaries to coincide with those of the county, to the incorporation of Caversham into Reading (and Berkshire) in 1911. Some of the changes related to truly eccentric divisions from years past, such as parts of Wokingham, Hurst, Shinfield and Swallowfield being classified as detached portions of Wiltshire, until that anomaly was rectified in 1844.

It was in 1974 that Berkshire lost some 260 square miles (36 per cent) of its area and almost 20 per cent of its population, when it gave up all of the area north of the Ridgeway to Oxfordshire, including attractive historic towns such as Wallingford and Abingdon, and received in return Slough, Eton and some other minor parts of Buckinghamshire. I leave you to judge how fair a swap this was, for fear of offending readers in Slough. Since the big shake-up of 1974 there have been further, smaller adjustments. Colnbrook and Poyle joined Berkshire in 1995, as did parts of Mapledurham, and Eye & Dunsden in 1997.

So, to answer my original question, I intend to play fast and loose with the county boundaries – working mainly with the traditional nineteenth-century Berkshire, but incorporating material about the post-1974 county where it seems relevant (or more to the point, interesting), and straying beyond even those boundaries when it seems to me that something worth reporting impinges upon life in modern Berkshire.

2

JUST PASSING THROUGH: TRANSPORT IN BERKSHIRE'S HISTORY

ROADS, ANCIENT AND MODERN

Part of England's, and possibly Europe's, oldest road runs through Berkshire. For 5,000 years, or more according to some authorities, the Icknield Way has provided traders with a drier and less forested (and hence safer) route between the Dorset coast and the Wash, in Norfolk. Iron Age forts were built along its length to protect this trade. In later years, its main function was as a drovers' road, taking large numbers of sheep to market in places like East Ilsley, near Newbury. (East Ilsley was in 1844 the largest sheep market in England, outside Smithfield.) The part of the Icknield Way running across the Berkshire Downs divided into a higher route along the ridge of the Downs, predictably called the Ridgeway, which crossed the Thames at Goring/Streatley, and a parallel lower route, the Icknield Way itself. The Ridgeway was designated a National Trail in 1973.

As we saw, Roman Berkshire was not a recognisable administrative area, and it was not even a significant channel of communication – there are roads out of neighbouring Silchester, heading north in the direction of Dorchester, east to London (which barely scratches the edge of modern Berkshire) and west to Cirencester, but no settlements of any size within the county itself.

Some of the earliest references to transport in Berkshire relate to unwelcome visitors. In AD 869, two Danish Viking armies made for the area, one sailing up the Thames and another marching overland down the Ridgeway. They met at Reading, where the confluence of the Thames and Kennet rivers provided routes to the north, east and west, and where they were able to occupy a former West Saxon fortress at the junction of the two rivers. By AD 871 they were firmly established in their base and, after a number of skirmishes, their army was defeated by that of the West Saxons at the Battle of Ashdown (dealt with in more detail in chapter 8).

In post-Roman times, towns on river crossings became increasingly important in shaping trade routes. Bridges at Abingdon, Wallingford, Henley and Maidenhead became key points in developing more direct westerly routes out of London. Others linked the Cotswolds, and their wool exports, to the channel ports. No less than five new bridges across the Thames were built during the thirteenth century, including Caversham, which dates from 1231, Maidenhead (built prior to 1255), Henley and Marlow. Windsor's bridge was older still – tolls from it were being collected as early as 1172.

There would tend to be a chapel on some bridges, like the one at St Anne's at Caversham, or a resident hermit to collect alms (as at the Ock Bridge in Abingdon). Charities or religious institutions might also collect tolls towards the upkeep of the bridges.

In Reading, responsibility for the upkeep of the Thames Bridge was shared between Reading and its neighbouring (but at that time independent) settlement of Caversham. They could never agree

about repair works, with the result that it spent centuries in a state of almost continuous disrepair, for a long time in a curious 'half and half' structure, partly of wood, partly of stone. In any event, tolls often put bridges beyond the means of the poorest travellers, who had to continue relying on ferries or (where feasible) fording rivers.

Between the bridges, mediaeval highways were rights of passage, rather than structures with fixed routes, and travellers would take whatever route was necessary to make progress. This may help explain why the very earliest maps did not show the roads between towns, given that their alignments were so uncertain.

If the poor condition of the roads was not enough, the misery was compounded by the fear of robbery. This had become so bad by 1285 that Edward I ordered that highways between market towns

King Edward I

should be widened so that there would be no ditch, undergrowth or bushes, where anyone could lurk with evil intent, within 200ft on either side of the road.

This only applied to a few major roads, and there were constant disputes as to who was responsible for maintenance of particular roads. In Reading after the dissolution of the Abbey, responsibility for their upkeep passed to the corporation (but not the resources to do anything about it). They fell into worse than usual disrepair, until a 1560 charter from Queen Elizabeth gave them both the responsibility and the means (financial and material – including the gift of 200 loads of stone from the ruins of Reading Abbey) to carry out the repairs.

A grossly inefficient parish-based unpaid labour system for repairing roads was introduced in 1555. It proved utterly inadequate to cope with the increased traffic trying to use them.

Celia Fiennes, in 1690, described the road from Reading to Theale as a 'sad clay deep way' and to Newbury was all 'clay mirey ground'. Wagons could sink axle-deep in mud, and in places the track was not wide enough for two carriages to pass. This road was nonetheless part of the Great Bath Road, probably the most important route in post-Roman Berkshire, forming a spine through the county linking London to the cities of Bath and Bristol.

This was not an ancient or even mediaeval creation, but was developed to carry the increasing traffic from the capital to the fashionable spa and the major port of Bristol. To say it was 'developed' may be overstating the case, since it was not even very clearly defined. It would regularly split into several different tracks, with no clear indication as to which was the right way to go (generally the higher route was the safer bet in wet weather). Travellers often even hired local guides; Samuel Pepys did not, and managed to get lost between Newbury and Reading.

Things had not looked up much by the time William Cobbett made his rural rides in 1822. He described the roads in the Windsor area as being mostly 'upon as bleak, as barren and as villainous a heath as ever man set eyes on'.

Nonetheless, the first stagecoach service through Berkshire was advertised in 1657. The vehicle was unsprung, carried only four people and took three days to complete the journey from London to Bath and Bristol, 'God willing' as the advertisement discouragingly put it. By the 1830s there were twenty-five stagecoaches and three Royal Mail coaches in each direction, running along the Bath Road through Maidenhead daily. Slough had twenty-four services, Reading seventeen, Newbury twelve, Hungerford ten, while Windsor got just four, Bracknell three and Wokingham two. In addition, there were cross-country services, for example linking Reading to Brighton, Oxford to Windsor, and Hungerford to Swindon.

The biggest maintenance problems faced those parishes that contained part of a long-distance route, like the Great Bath Road. Some way had to be found of making the long-distance traveller pay towards the wear and tear he caused on the highways. An answer came with the introduction of Turnpike Trusts. Private Acts of Parliament brought into being trusts that would replace the parishes as highway authority on specific routes. They were able to raise loans to fund highway improvements, which they repaid from the tolls paid by the users of the roads.

Turnpiking was a very slow and piecemeal way of upgrading a road, as the improvement of the Berkshire part of the Great Bath Road illustrates. The road from Reading to Theale was one of the first to be turnpiked (in 1714), followed by Twyford to Maidenhead (1718), west and east of Newbury (1726 and 1728), Cranford to Maidenhead (1727) and Twyford to Reading (1736). Other Berkshire roads to be turnpiked at this time included Maidenhead to Henley Bridge (1718), Reading to Basingstoke (1718), Reading to Wallingford (1763), Newbury to Oxford via Abingdon (1770), Hungerford to Wantage and Fyfield (*c*. 1795) and Windsor to Hurst (1823).

So, by the start of the nineteenth century, a reasonable network of turnpiked roads existed between most significant settlements in the county. Each trust had to justify to Parliament that the turnpike was needed (not so difficult, given the appalling state of so many roads) and that the scale of charges they were proposing was justified by the financial outlay needed to improve and maintain the road. Turnpike proposals were generally hotly contested, since the placing of a tollgate could determine who had to pay to reach a key destination and who did not.

Once established, there was widespread evasion and fraud to contend with. Landowners would conspire with travellers to enable them to circumnavigate the barriers, and all sorts of ingenious ways were found to reduce the tolls for which travellers were liable. The tariffs themselves were exceedingly complex, with different rules applying according to the weight of your load, the shape, height and width of the wagon wheels and the form of motive power (steam road vehicles, once they came along, faced punitive tariffs from some trusts).

The Maidenhead Trust was one of the first to have its own weighing machine for wagons. There were also numerous complicated exemptions to the tariffs – for pedestrians, funerals, churchgoers, horses going to water, members of the Royal Family, etc.

Trusts were also entitled to a share of the unpaid labour that still looked after the non-turnpiked roads in the parish. But this was by no means easily obtained, given that the parishes still struggled to maintain even local routes (since turnpikes never made up more than a fifth of the total road network). Trusts often had to resort to the courts to get their share of the labour. As if all that were not enough, the complex tariffs gave the toll collectors considerable scope for in-house fraud, and their tollhouses were popular targets for highwaymen.

All in all, it is small wonder that turnpike roads – though they made significant improvements – were not a panacea for overland travel in Britain. They were still limited by the speed at which horses could travel, and even the speediest traffic – the mail coaches – were still taking twelve hours between London and Bristol in 1836. Goods carried by wagon or canal barge could take several days – longer, if the canals were closed down by frost or drought. When not bogged down in mud, the roads could also be extremely bumpy. The Marlow Road (the modern A404) was noted as being less rough than the Great Bath Road, and for that reason was favoured by the likes of the Marquis of Salisbury, for being easier on his gout. It became known as the 'gout track'. As for The Great Bath Road, the *Gentlemen's Magazine* for September 1754, after listing a long schedule of the route's shortcomings, called it '… the worst public road in Europe, considering what vast sums have been collected from it.'

The turnpikes were badly hit by the coming of the railways. In 1844 the Windsor Forest Turnpike earned £743 in tolls. In 1850, the year after the railway came to Wokingham, this fell to £414. By 1870 all the turnpike trusts had closed. Further major improvements to the county's roads would only come with the widespread use of Macadam's road building technique in the nineteenth century; pressure from the cycling and the motor car lobbies, especially after the county councils took over responsibility for road maintenance from the parishes in 1888; and the discovery of tar as a means of defeating dust early in the twentieth century. As late as the First World War, the Bath Road was still being described as a mess of potholes and loose gravel, with warning signs to alert travellers to the worst hazards, though it was by then being reconstructed.

By the 1920s, the volume of motor traffic had increased to the point of becoming a nuisance, and Twyford and Colnbrook were two of the first settlements in Berkshire to be bypassed. This also had the advantage of creating work for demobbed ex-servicemen.

Having started with Britain's oldest road, we move on to one of Berkshire's newest. The need for a 'South Wales motorway', as they originally called it, was first identified in the 1930s. At first the authorities thought that a series of bypasses of the major towns along the route, which could then be joined up in some way, would suffice, but it was soon realised that this would not achieve the standard of road or the directness of route required. Consulting engineers were called in, and seven alternative routes were looked at, at one time or another, in the 1950s and 1960s. The southernmost one went south of Reading, Newbury and Hungerford; the northernmost one way to the north of Didcot and Swindon. In finest British tradition the authorities dithered, as the engineers tried to reconcile directness and construction costs with amenity, while comparing routes that variously ploughed through the Thames Valley, the Chilterns, the Berkshire Downs, the Savernake Forest and the Marlborough Uplands, and lobbyists lobbied furiously against the route they were looking to protect.

In 1969 it was announced that the M4 (as it was now called) was about to start construction – by which time it was very sorely needed indeed. East–west through traffic was still having to go through the centre of all the towns en route, and the A4 was carrying somewhere between two and three times the number of vehicles for which it had been designed. At busy times like holiday periods, traffic queues built up for several miles either side of towns like Reading, with motorists taking an hour and a half to reach the other side of town.

The M4 was finally to be opened in December 1971, by a junior minister at the Environment Department – one Michael Heseltine – driving down it in the ministerial Jaguar. A ceremony was held, in which the Bishop of Oxford blessed the road, but the ministerial Jaguar – no doubt feeling unblessed – then refused to start. So Mr Heseltine climbed into the ministerial coach for the trip.

The opening period was not without incident. At one point motorists found themselves mingling on the carriageway with the hounds and huntsmen of the Duke of Beaufort's hunt, after a fox ignored the 'no entry' signs. Debris left on the road by the contractors meant that replacement windscreen suppliers did a roaring trade, and the lack of services anywhere between west

London and the Severn Bridge kept breakdown services busy filling empty petrol tanks.

Road schemes generally seem to be like fine wines, in that they cannot be hurried. Even the relatively modest matter of an A4 bypass to Maidenhead was first proposed in 1927. A route was surveyed and work actually began in the 1930s. But it was interrupted by the war, and further delayed by post-war austerity. The scheme was only revived in 1959 and opened in June 1961.

But the most leisurely of all must surely be the third Thames crossing at Reading. A joint committee for the orderly expansion of Greater Reading was convened by authorities in Berkshire and Oxfordshire in 1928. The need for the bridge was raised at that time and the proposal has surfaced at regular intervals ever since, but still remains no more than a fond hope in some hearts (and a nightmare in others).

RIVERS AND CANALS

Given the state of the roads, the nation's waterways formed important corridors of trade for much of its history. In Berkshire's case, the River Thames formed much of the county's northern boundary and provided routes eastwards and northwards, while the River Kennet flowed through the western part of Berkshire. Reading assumed a special importance in two ways: first as a place to tranship goods arriving by road from the surrounding area, for delivery to London via the Thames; and secondly as a place for transferring goods, going up the Kennet to western Berkshire, into shallow- drafted boats, called 'showtes'. These were the only craft that could navigate the unimproved Kennet. The abbey controlled access to the Kennet by means of a lock, and charged users for it, and a wharf and warehouse were also provided in the twelfth century, near to where the Holy Brook joins the Kennet.

As with most waterways at that time, there were constant disputes between those who wanted to use the river for transport, on the one hand, and fishermen and watermill owners, on the other. The latter in particular would build weirs (or flash locks) across the river, and boatmen would have to pay (and wait) for them to be opened. They would then either be hauled upstream through the opened dam by cables or surf downstream on the rapids. This was not only extremely inefficient but dangerous – the flash lock at Marlow, owned by a man called Thomas Farmer, had a particularly evil reputation for drowning its users.

Successive kings legislated in vain against the damming of rivers. It was only with the development of modern-style pound locks (invented in Holland in 1373, and first used in Britain in 1566) that the two interests could be reconciled.

(As an aside, Jerome K. Jerome reported a similar rivalry between river users in the form of rowers and punters versus steam launches. Oarsmen hated the steamers and would go out of their way to annoy them.)

The idea of linking London and Bristol via the rivers Thames, Kennet and Avon had been around since Elizabethan times. It came close to happening in 1626, but for the untimely death of the man who had surveyed the Kennet and Avon and who had seen the potential. But, before that could happen, the Kennet Navigation Act (1715) was passed, to make the Kennet between Reading and Newbury navigable (despite the fall of 120ft between the two towns).

At Newbury, the building of a canal basin and a wharf involved demolishing a Norman castle. All the towns along the route supported the idea except Reading, who feared that they would lose their pre-eminent trading position. In 1720 this opposition spiralled into violence, when a mob of about 300 people, led by Mayor Robert Blake, attempted to destroy part of the canal works. They were unsuccessful but, thanks to the incompetence of the first engineer employed by the canal company, they were deeply in debt by the time the navigation opened in 1723. They had had to bring a second engineer to put in 11½ miles of cuttings, to make the route direct enough to be competitive. The people of Reading added to their problems by stoning,

and making death threats to, bargees passing through the town. The company made almost no profits for the first twenty-five years but, far from bankrupting Reading, the canal ushered in a new era of prosperity for all the towns along it.

The long-awaited link between London and Bristol finally got parliamentary approval in 1794 and opened in 1810. This and other canal developments gave Berkshire excellent trading links with key parts of industrial Britain. But the glory days of the canals were to be short-lived, with the coming of the railways. In the first year of operation of the Great Western Railway, the Kennet and Avon's takings from lock tolls fell from £51,000 to £41,000. The railway bought out the canal in 1852, starting a predictable period of neglect and decline. As for the Wiltshire and Berkshire Canal (discussed in more detail in chapter 10), by 1870 it was already being described as 'a muddy trickle'. The Thames Commissioners, heavily in debt, were wound up in 1867 and replaced by the Thames Conservancy.

One piece of canal building that definitely post-dated the railway age was the Slough branch of the Grand Union Canal. This opened in 1882, and was used to transport bricks from the manufacturers in Iver and Langley to their market in London. On the return journey, the barges would bring London's refuse and night soil, the latter used to fertilise Slough's many market gardens. No doubt it also helped take locals' minds off the smells from the town's brickworks.

The modern British Waterways Board has long-term ambitions to construct a 2-mile link between the Slough arm of the Canal and the River Thames.

THE GREAT WESTERN RAILWAY

As the Liverpool to Manchester Railway opened in 1830, merchants in Bristol looked on enviously. They saw their two rival cities' economic prospects being transformed by the speed with which goods and people could be transported between them, and they decided to revive an idea which had first seen the light of day in 1824. In 1832 a 27-year-old engineer named Brunel was appointed to design a railway between Bristol and its main market, London. The route would inevitably go through large parts of historic Berkshire.

Like most early railway schemes, the scheme encountered entrenched opposition. Within Berkshire, this included the authorities in Maidenhead, who feared the railway would deny them valuable toll income from their Thames river crossing. (The bridge, built for £19,000 in 1772, had long since been paid for, but they kept charging tolls on it. This only stopped in 1903, after Parliament ruled them illegal and protesters threw the tollgates into the river.)

More substantial opposition to the railway appeared in the form of Eton College, who feared it would carry their pupils off to the fleshpots of the capital. They demanded that a large, guarded fence be erected along the 4 miles of track nearest to the college, and that Slough, the nearest town along the line, be barred from having a station. The fence was provided, but the station issue was easily solved – the railway initially pretended that the station serving Slough would be at Langley, beyond the fenced-off zone. In practice, they hired rooms in a trackside public house in the centre of Slough, which they used as a waiting room from which passengers could decant onto the track itself to board their train. The town then only had to wait until June 1840, when a change in the law allowed a proper station to be built.

In similar vein, the University of Oxford and its chancellor, the Duke of Wellington (who was no fan of railways), refused at first to have a station nearer to Oxford than Steventon, 10 miles south of the city, adding an hour and a half to the journey time between

Oxford and London. The Thames Commissioners, fearful of a loss of river-borne trade, instructed their general committee to 'take all such steps as they shall deem advisable for effectually opposing the progress of this useless and mischievous project'.

Landowners around Reading complained of 'the destruction of land, the asseverance of enclosures, the inundation of foreign labourers, and the increased poor rate' and told Parliament that the railway would be 'injurious to their interests, repugnant to their feelings, and that no case of public utility had been made out to justify such an uncalled for encroachment upon the rights of private property'. A correspondent to the local newspaper doubted whether Reading could benefit from a railway: 'Here there is no manufacture, nor is it within the range of possibility that any can flourish here; nor can the trade of the place be improved; it now supplies the country around with everything, and more it cannot do.'

Despite the opposition, and the fact that a first, partial scheme was thrown out by Parliament, the Great Western Railway Bill was finally approved in August 1835.

The biggest engineering challenges Brunel faced in the Berkshire part of the Great Western were the Thames crossing at Maidenhead and the Sonning Cutting. The geography of the Maidenhead bridge site was such that Brunel was forced to span the river using the shallowest brick arches ever seen. All the 'experts' predicted that it would collapse, but it still stands to this day, carrying far heavier and faster trains than were ever envisaged in his day.

At Sonning, Brunel was faced with making a cutting 2 miles long and up to 60ft deep, all of it dug by men using just picks and shovels. He had up to 1,200 navvies working for more than three years in a sea of mud to complete this mammoth task. At one stage, the contractor ran out of money to pay the workmen; they went on strike and took to hanging around the streets of Reading, so terrifying the locals that the army had to be called out for their protection.

Other great engineering challenges faced Brunel further along his route – notably the Box Tunnel – but the railway opened throughout the length of Berkshire by the end of 1840, and to Bristol in June, 1841.

Once the railway began operating, all but the most die-hard sceptics could see its advantages. Branch lines followed – from Reading to Newbury and Hungerford in 1847, and to Basingstoke in 1848. Even towns that had petitioned against a railway had a change of heart. Abingdon, which was at that time the county town, had twice opposed the railway. But by 1842 they were lobbying the Great Western for the branch line, which was by then being mooted to Oxford, to come closer to them. Negotiations with Abingdon broke down, and it was left to a local company to supply their branch line, in 1856. However, the town remained on the fringes of the rail network, and this is reflected in its subsequent lack of growth.

After much negotiation with Eton College and others, Windsor was finally served by not one, but two, branch lines in 1849. Newbury, not satisfied just with a branch line from Reading, campaigned to extend its line north to Didcot and south to Southampton, and this opened in 1882.

Queen Victoria started her first train ride from Slough in 1842 and a palatial hotel was built opposite the station, to act as her private waiting room for future journeys and to serve the many who would be drawn to Windsor by the royal presence. Its days were numbered from the day the branch lines to Windsor itself got the go-ahead.

The last London to Bristol stagecoach ran in 1843, and with their passing went the businesses of the many coaching inns. But towns like Maidenhead, which had had an important coaching trade, found that its loss was more than compensated for by new coaching business generated by the railways. As we saw, the waterways were much harder hit.

The Sonning cutting was to play an unexpected and macabre part in railway history. On Christmas Eve 1841, heavy rain caused a landslip in the cutting. At about 6.40 a.m. a mixed goods and third-class passenger train entered the cutting and crashed into the debris. The third-class 'carriages' were no more than low-sided open wagons and many of the passengers were either thrown from them or crushed by the train of goods wagons behind them. Eight were killed and seventeen injured were taken to the new Royal Berkshire Hospital. The outrage that this accident caused led to William Gladstone's 1844 Railway Regulations Act – the government's important first attempt to regulate the conditions under which poorer passengers travelled and the cost of their travel.

The original stations at Slough and Reading had the unusual feature that they were 'one-sided' (that is, both the up and down platforms were next to each other, on the same side of the track). The logic of this was that virtually all of the two towns lay on that side of the tracks. However, it made for some complicated and dangerous crossing movements and the experiment was abandoned.

Parts of the Berkshire rail network have been lost over the years. The Marlow branch from Maidenhead used to go as far as Oxford. The Didcot, Newbury and Southampton line closed in 1973, and that from Newbury to Lambourn went the same year. The branch from Cholsey to Wallingford went in 1981, the Oxford line to Abingdon in 1963, and the Faringdon branch from Uffington closed in 1973. The Wantage branch, originally a tramway, carried goods traffic until its closure in 1946. Reading's goods branch to Coley yard closed in 1983, and part of it is now the line of the A33 relief road.

TRAMS AND BUSES

The introduction of bus services to Berkshire might be said to date back to the 1840s, when stagecoach proprietors, losing their established business to the railways, took to providing feeder coach services to the railway stations. Enterprising innkeepers also laid on services between the stations and their establishments. The proprietor of the Peacock Inn in Reading's Broad Street went one stage further, providing services to Caversham (terminating at the Prince of Wales), Cemetery Junction (the Marquis of Granby) and Christchurch Road, Whitley (the Queen's Head).

The Tramways Act of 1870 opened the way for tram services to come to Reading. The Reading Tramways Company (a subsidiary of the Imperial Tramways Company) got permission to build a 2¼ mile horse drawn tramway between Brock Barracks on Oxford Road and Cemetery Junction (then just about the two limits of Reading's built-up area).

This came into operation in 1879 and, after some teething problems, was soon carrying some 14,000 passengers a week. The company had to increase the frequency of services and bring in double-decker trams. They ran until 1901, when the Corporation exercised its right to buy out the (by then clapped out) service for the grand sum of £11,394. They immediately began electrifying it, and on 22 July 1903 huge crowds turned out in Reading town centre to witness the inauguration of the new service.

The original route gradually grew into a network that became part of the fabric of the town for the next thirty years. By that time, the trams were seen to be too slow (16mph) and too inflexible, and from the 1930s they began to be replaced by trolley buses and petrol buses. The last tram ran on 20 May 1939 (just months before the outbreak of war with its petrol shortages – bad timing). As for the trolley buses, which a 1930s timetable described as 'the last word in comfort – "first-class" travel at "third-class" fares', Reading continued to expand its network until 1963, at a time when many towns were phasing theirs out. Reading was one of the last six authorities in the country to scrap its trolley buses, the final service running on 3 November 1968.

Petrol buses made their first appearance in Berkshire during the First World War. A service ran from the Bear public house in Maidenhead to central Reading and on to Streatley in July 1915, operating from a depot in Caversham Road, Reading. For much of the journey, the buses stopped wherever asked to do so by the passengers. In those war years women took the place of men as conductors (they were quickly replaced by males after the war finished), and all the staff had to work long hours of compulsory overtime to keep the services on the road. An eighty-hour working week was typical.

Not only staff, but also buses and petrol were in short supply. Their first vehicles came (very) second-hand from Barnsley and District Transport. They did, however, have such unheard of luxuries as electric lighting and padded seats. Two of the other early vehicles were simply open lorries with garden seats fixed in the back, and another of their vehicles had a roof but no glazed windows, just canvas blinds that could be rolled down in the event of bad weather. Only the flood of government surplus vehicles that came onto the market after the war overcame the shortage. It was no easy task, maintaining a reliable service with these primitive vehicles. They had no electric starters and it could take three people to hand-crank them on cold mornings. Also, in the days before anti-freeze, radiators had to be drained overnight whenever frost threatened.

As for wartime petrol shortages, some of the first buses were converted to run on gas, carrying huge inflatable sacks of it about on the roof, which they refilled from specially adapted gas lamp standards. For all their bulk, these only provided the equivalent of 2 gallons of petrol; in addition, the gas bags fouled on trees as they went past; the gas powered buses were down on power; and the timetables also had to be altered to allow for frequent refilling of the bag. Even gas supplies to the bus company were eventually rationed. Experiments were also made, with eking out of the petrol supply by adding paraffin to it.

Despite all the shortages, many new services were added during the war years. One, to Cliveden, involved climbing a steep hill, and the conductress had to be ready with a large wooden wedge to put behind the wheel of the bus, should it grind to a halt and threaten to roll backwards. One conductress lost several fingers trying to do so.

Another took visitors from Reading to the Berkshire Lunatic Asylum. Return tickets were issued at the Reading end, to try and make it harder for the inmates to use the bus as a means of escape.

But many services also had to be cut, and not always due to fuel shortages. The Restricted Lighting Order 1916, an early form of blackout, only allowed vehicles to travel on sidelights after dark. This made it too dangerous to operate country routes at night, as was demonstrated when a 75-year-old deaf lady from Twyford and a bus driver on sidelights failed to notice each other, with fatal consequences for the lady.

In addition to the specialist bus operators, one of the most important bus services in the area at this time was operated by a Henley grocer, Edwin Venn-Brown. These did not necessarily operate every day, but were tied to the market days in different towns.

BERKSHIRE AVIATION

For almost thirty years, Berkshire had its own airfield and aircraft industry, based at Woodley, near Reading. It was established by two motorbike sales and repair businessmen, named Phillips and Powis. Charles Powis became hooked on flying after he and his wife flew to France for a holiday in 1928. He took lessons and qualified as a pilot in the following year, and very soon afterwards got an agency to sell de Havilland Moths and Simmonds Spartans, two popular light aircraft of the day. They also acquired a piece of land called the 'Hundred Acre Field' at Woodley, as an airfield, which opened in February 1929. Lock-up garages were provided for planes with folding wings, and a single hangar for the others. It was here, in December 1931, that the wartime fighter ace Douglas Bader had the plane crash that would cost him his legs.

Phillips' and Powis' careers as aircraft manufacturers, as opposed to sellers, began in 1932, when they teamed up with a talented and innovatory young designer called Frederick Miles, to build a new aircraft, the Hawk. By 1934 they were selling one a week, and one came second in the 1934 King's Cup air race. As war approached, the Hawk was taken on as an RAF trainer and Miles also developed an advanced trainer, the Kestrel, to provide trainees with a transition to the likes of the Spitfire. The Air Ministry placed a £2 million order for a modified version of the Kestrel and, by September 1940, 500 had been delivered.

Throughout the war, Miles continued to produce radical designs, from a cut price substitute for the Hurricane fighter, to a post-war transatlantic airliner in which passengers could sit in comfortable lounges, as opposed to serried ranks; from the Aerovan, which resembled nothing so much as a flying Ford Transit, to the M.52 supersonic jet research plane, which would have been capable of up to 1,000mph in a dive. The designs for this latter model were given to the Americans in part payment of our war debts, and went on to influence the design of their supersonic record-breaking Bell X-1.

But peace came, and with it ruin for Miles. Most of their military orders were cancelled, and the government was too unadventurous

to take on his radical peacetime projects. In 1947 their company was taken over by Britain's oldest aircraft manufacturer, Handley Page. They continued to operate from Woodley and built a development of a Miles design, which became known as the Handley Page Herald. It was a replacement for the wartime Douglas DC-3 Dakota, and first flew in 1955, but was beaten into production by its Dutch rival the Fokker Friendship. By 1963 only thirty-five Heralds had been sold and the company finally went into liquidation at the end of the 1960s.

3

BERKSHIRE MURDERS

Most people enjoy a good murder (provided it is happening to someone else) and Berkshire has had enough of them to fill several anthologies. I am indebted to these for much – but not all – of what follows, and would encourage all armchair murder enthusiasts to follow up the specialist sources for a more detailed account of these and other foul deeds.

THE SWEENEY TODD OF COLNBROOK

Our story begins with some of the oldest murders, and one with many variations in the different accounts of the story, which I have tried to reflect below. The Ostrich Inn, Colnbrook, dates from 1106 (according to some sources – others claim that the building and historical records relating to it do not go back any further than the sixteenth century). However old it is, it is thought to have been the site of over sixty murders. Most of them are attributed to a couple called Jarman, who were licensees during the seventeenth (or possibly the fourteenth, or even twelfth) century and who are said to have been the model for the character of Sweeney Todd, the demon barber of Fleet Street (one of several claimants of that dubious distinction).

The inn was used as a stopover by coaches and other travellers and the Jarmans would look out for well-heeled solitary guests. Having plied them with strong liquor and seen them to bed in their best 'blue room', they would open a trapdoor which tipped them from their bed into a vat of boiling water (or possibly oil) that finished them off. They disposed of the bodies and helped themselves to the victim's valuables. Their career came to an end when they murdered a wealthy merchant from Reading, named Thomas Cole (or Coln, or was it somebody surnamed Thomas?), but forgot to dispose of his horse (or was it a donkey?). The animal was found, leading to a search for Cole, whose body was found in a nearby stream.

(According to one version, the stream had an unusually low flow on this occasion, and failed to carry the body away, as it had the previous victims.)

The Jarmans were arrested, tried and hanged for fifteen counts of murder, though Jarman confessed (boasted?) to his gaoler that the real number had been more like sixty. There is even a suggestion that the name Colnbrook derives from this final murder – Cole-in-the-brook. A nice story, but Colnbrook features in Domesday Book, which rather pre-dates Mr Cole, whichever version of the story you believe.

It is also said that one of the licensees of the Hind's Head Inn, in Bracknell, tried to copy the Jarmans' murderous ways, until he, too, was caught, tried and executed.

DANGEROUS WORK, FARMING

The next two examples illustrate that farming could be dangerous work, especially when you were travelling home from market alone, and were thought to be carrying the proceeds from a day's business.

Jacob Saunders, born in Reading in about 1700, was a bad lot from the start. He would not learn a trade or get a job, and was constantly getting into trouble. One day in 1722, he learned that a local farmer called Blagrave was in town engaging in some large-scale financial transactions, and he decided that there might be a nice little earner in it for him. Blagrave lingered at the Catherine Wheel pub after finishing his business and Saunders fell briefly into conversation with him there.

It was almost midnight when Blagrave set off to walk to his home in Caversham, and Saunders followed him. At a suitably rural and isolated point in the journey, Saunders overtook Blagrave and attacked him with a heavy piece of timber. Once he thought that Blagrave was dead, Saunders went through his pockets, but was disappointed to find only a few pence in them. He vented his anger by beating Blagrave some more, before returning home, where his wife found his behaviour odd.

Blagrave actually survived for several days before expiring, but was never able to give an account of the attack. However, Saunders' conversation with Blagrave in the pub had not gone unnoticed by some of the other customers. He had left the pub at about the same time as Blagrave, and people other than his wife had noticed a change in his demeanour in the days that followed. It was enough for the mayor to issue a warrant for Saunders' arrest, and he was detained whilst leaving church.

At first, he denied all knowledge of the crime, while giving an unconvincing account of his whereabouts that night. But after an unsuccessful attempt to escape from custody, he admitted some involvement but tried falsely to implicate two other 'bad lots' in the actual murder, in the hope of leniency for himself. They were arrested and tried for murder, but proved to have cast-iron alibis.

Saunders was sentenced to be hung in chains near to the spot where the murder took place, and died on a tree at Gallows Tree Common, near Caversham, in March 1723.

John Dormer was born in 1779 to a poor but honest family in High Wycombe. He was apprenticed to a bricklayer at the age of 15 and married at 18, but a year later deserted both wife and employer, running off to Portsmouth to become a marine. The life did not suit him (for several reasons, including chronic seasickness) and six months later he absconded, becoming a fugitive who supported himself by petty crime. He fell into a criminal partnership with Richard Alder from Marlow.

By July 1801 they had acquired firearms and hatched a plan to rob a mail coach at Maidenhead Thicket. The robbery was bungled, as the coach driver saw them coming and was able to whip his horses into a gallop to evade them. As a consolation prize, the pair decided to rob one of the farmers returning from Maidenhead market instead. A farmer named Robinson was the chosen victim but, when they demanded his money or his life, he made the wrong choice, telling them that they should work for a living. They shot him dead.

However, the pair had been overheard plotting their crime in a local inn, and the authorities, furnished with an accurate description of them, soon had them in custody. However, the evidence against them was only circumstantial and so they set about trying to get one of them to turn King's evidence against the other. Dormer remained resolutely loyal to his partner, denying all knowledge of the crime, but Alder sold Dormer down the river. He told the police that he had thought they were simply flagging farmer Robinson down to ask for a lift, when Dormer had produced a gun and shot him. This implausible tale was nonetheless a convenient way for the authorities to secure a conviction. Alder walked free, while Dormer was sentenced to death at Abingdon Assizes.

In his last days, Dormer was described as 'a changed man, frightened and ashamed and pleading with God for forgiveness'. He also told the court (rather too late) that it had been Alder who fired

the fatal shot. He went to the gallows at Reading in July 1801, before suffering the added indignity of having his body publicly dissected by surgeons at Reading town hall.

Other witnesses later recalled how they had heard Alder drunkenly boasting about how he had got away with murder.

TRAPPED BY TECHNOLOGY

Our next murder is one of the first examples of a suspect being caught with the aid of new technology. John Tawell was a personable and, to all outward appearances, respectable man. He had a successful business and was apparently a pious pillar of the church. He was a Quaker, and had married a wealthy Quaker widow. What was not widely known was that he had been sentenced to transportation for fraud as a young man.

He also had a taste for extra-marital affairs. One of these was with a woman named Sarah Hart, a former servant of his, whom he set up in a cottage in Slough and by whom he fathered two children. The relationship began to sour when Tawell retired, but the resulting decline in his income was not matched by Sarah's propensity for spending it.

By 1 January 1845, the relationship was well beyond sour. Tawell went to visit her armed with supplies of prussic acid, some of which he poured into Sarah's stout. Their loud arguments were followed by Sarah's screams of pain, and Tawell was seen fleeing from Sarah's house in the direction of the railway station. A neighbour, hearing Sarah's cries, went to her aid. The doctor was called, along with a priest, and the latter recalled seeing Tawell catch the train back to Paddington.

They were too late to save her, or to stop him, but in 1842 the Great Western Railway had installed one of the new-fangled telegraph machines along the line from Paddington to Slough. Its main purpose was to send safety messages to assist in the running of the railway, and the priest soon persuaded them to telegraph Paddington, informing them of Tawell's crime, and notifying them of his likely time of arrival. Police met Tawell's train at Paddington, tracked him back to his lodgings and next day they arrested him. At his trial in March 1845 it took the jury just half an hour to convict him of murder.

Tawell was hanged at Aylesbury (Slough then being part of Buckinghamshire) on 28 March 1845 and the Great Western Railway established a first in solving crime with the help of this new technology.

BABY AND CHILD KILLERS

The last man to be given a public hanging in Berkshire was a hod carrier from Clewer, near Windsor, called John Gould. Gould had a track (and criminal) record of violent and quarrelsome behaviour and, on 30 December 1861, finding there was no call for hod carrying at that time of year, retired to the Prince of Wales public house for the morning. He left behind his 7-year-old daughter, Hannah, in the care of a neighbour. When he returned, the worse for wear, in mid-afternoon, he found that Hannah had failed to tidy the house to his satisfaction or light the fire. Flying into an uncontrollable rage, Gould cut his daughter's throat with a razor and flung the child out into the street. She died as horrified neighbours carried her to hospital. The police came and, after a struggle, arrested Gould.

He was, shortly afterwards, led through hissing crowds at Windsor Station for the journey to Reading Gaol and his trial at the Assizes.

The case opened to a packed house, including many 'persons of genteel appearance' and 'a considerable sprinkle of females'. He pleaded guilty and his counsel questioned witnesses in search of evidence of insanity that might mitigate the offence.

At his trial, fellow drinkers reported how, in his drunken state, Gould had intimated that he was going to murder someone (he had not named the intended victim) but that no one had paid it much attention. As for Gould himself, he could only express regret for his actions and blame them on the demon drink. Once he had been drinking, he told the court, he didn't know what he was about.

The jury reached a unanimous verdict of guilty within ten minutes. Perhaps surprisingly, strenuous efforts were made to appeal against the verdict, a group of Berkshire gentlemen even travelling to London to plead for his life with the home secretary. However, the executioner was booked for 14 March 1862 and Gould was allowed to give his fellow prisoners some final words of advice. Unsurprisingly, he told them to abstain from drunkenness.

His execution attracted a huge crowd, including many women and children. It would be another six years before legislation required all future executions to be conducted in private, but it was the last chance the people of Berkshire would have to witness the gruesome spectacle of a public hanging.

One child killer so horrified Victorian society that they earned themselves a place, not just on the gallows but also in Madame

Tussaud's House of Horrors. In those days, the shame of having a child out of wedlock, or sheer economic necessity, could force people to look for someone else to bring up their child as their own, in return for payment. The occupation of baby farmer evolved – not respectable or even legal, but an established fact of life.

In September 1895, a couple named Arthur and Mary Anne (known as Polly) Palmer moved from Cardiff to Caversham, bringing with them Polly's mother, Amelia (known as Annie) Dyer. The family were badly in debt and Annie had a history of mental instability, including several more or less unconvincing suicide attempts. Annie also had a criminal record for baby farming that stretched back to 1880. Once in Caversham, she renewed her activities, advertising herself as a wealthy farmer's wife. She took in eleven babies over a very short period and, by April 1896, four of them were dead.

The body of one was fished out of the Thames by a bargeman on 30 March and, by the end of April, seven tiny bodies had been recovered from the river. They had all been strangled with white tape, and one of them was wrapped in brown paper. The paper bore the address in Piggott's Road, Caversham, where Annie had lived, and the name Mrs Thomas, one of the aliases she used. The false name and the fact that she had subsequently moved delayed the police in finding her, but only for a while.

She was tried in May for the murder of just one of the infants, and entered a plea of insanity. The court was regaled with lurid tales of birds talking to her, other voices telling her to kill herself and her bed seeming to sink through the floor. It did her no good; the jury took just five minutes to find her both sane and guilty, and she was hanged at Newgate Prison on 10 June 1896.

The case caused a sensation at the time. The papers contained detailed (and largely invented) accounts of her last moments, and parents would threaten errant children with being sent into the care of Mrs Dyer. A sale of her meagre personal effects attracted a huge crowd, including numbers of fairground sideshow proprietors, eager to cash in on her notoriety. Nobody knows to this day how many babies Dyer murdered in the course of her 'career'. Four years after her death, four more infant bodies were found buried in the garden of a house in Bristol in which she had once lived. Her fate did not deter her daughter and son-in-law. In September 1898 the pair of them were arrested for farming (and immediately abandoning) a baby.

THE CONDEMNED CELL IN NEWGATE.

MURDEROUS BALLADS

In the days when the execution of murderers was much more of a spectator sport, an early example of merchandising took the form of ballads, commemorating the foul deed, which were sold at trials and (until they were abolished) public executions. Here we look at two Berkshire examples of the genre. The first leaves you wondering whether the sublimely awful Scottish poet, William McGonagall, had a second career as a balladeer. The second is written by a much more distinguished hand.

Poaching was rife in an area north of Hungerford in 1876 and, one night in December, Inspector Joseph Drewett and Constable Thomas Shorter were out hunting for the perpetrators. When they failed to return, another constable was dispatched to find them. What he found was the blood-stained body of Shorter, and then, nearby, that of Drewett. Both had been battered and shot at close range. A local gamekeeper reported seeing two well-known local figures pass the nearby turnpike gate. One, a labourer named William Day, was thought to be the leader of a poaching gang. The other was his son-in-law, William Tidbury. The pair of them, plus two of Tidbury's brothers, were promptly arrested.

There was no shortage of evidence against them. Footprints matching theirs were found at the scene of the murders; their clothes and hands still had blood on them and broken gun parts found at the scene corresponded to weapons they owned. The case caused a sensation. The court hearing at Berkshire Assizes attracted such a large crowd that police control was needed and the event had to be made ticket only. With the crowds came the balladeers, and just the chorus of this one should be enough for you to judge its literary merits:

> Near Hungerford in Berkshire, on a lonely roadside,
> Two policemen by a murder so cruel they died;
> Quite dead and cold they were both of them found,
> Their brains beaten out as they lay on the ground.

In the event, it was William Tidbury's two brothers, Francis and Henry, who were found guilty of the murders and subsequently hanged at Reading Gaol in March 1877.

The second balladeer was none other than Oscar Wilde who, in 1896, was residing at Reading Gaol, following his conviction for homosexual offences. His 'Ballad of Reading Gaol' tells the story of a trooper, Charles T. Wooldridge. He was a serving soldier with the Royal Horse Guards, with an exemplary service record but a failing marriage. This was not helped by the fact that he was based at barracks in London, while his wife, Laura, lived at Clewer, near Windsor.

Laura was said to have had an eye for the men, though how far this was just in the fevered imagination of her husband was not entirely clear. Wooldridge took to visiting her unexpectedly, in hopes of catching her in flagrante delicto. His visits began to lead to blazing rows and, by March 1896, to physical violence, when he punched her repeatedly in the face (an unprepossessing side to him that does not come out in Wilde's ballad). Wooldridge later wrote to Laura, professing undying love but accepting that they could no longer live together in harmony.

Initially he said they should never meet again but, by the end of March, he turned up at her house in Clewer, demanding to see her. She reluctantly let him in and the predictable row ensued. There were screams, and moments later Laura's body was found in the road outside, her throat slashed. Wooldridge had disappeared, but reappeared at Windsor police station shortly afterwards, where he confessed to the crime. He changed his plea to not guilty at the trial and his lawyer tried to argue that it was a crime of passion at a moment when he had temporarily taken leave of his senses (which is essentially the line taken in Wilde's ballad).

It was to no avail. The prosecution proved that he had borrowed the razor used in the murder the night before, which suggested a degree of premeditation. A 'guilty' verdict and a sentence of death followed, and Wooldridge was executed at Reading Gaol in July 1896. Wilde wrote the ballad in France in 1897, after his release from prison, and it was published the following year under the *nom de plume* C.3.3 (Wilde's cell block, landing and cell). Even without his celebrity name attached it became a considerable success, going through seven printings in a year. Its most famous lines are:

> And all men kill the thing they love
> By all let this be heard
> Some do it with a bitter look
> Some with a flattering word
> The coward does it with a kiss
> The brave man with a sword.

If the sale of ballads was a relatively innocuous example of merchandising on the back of murder, a much more gruesome example occurred after the White Hart murder, at Wantage in 1833. In this, an itinerant fruit picker called George King hacked off the head of Ann Pullen, the licensee of the White Hart. Pullen's mother turned her daughter's headless and bloodied body into a grisly exhibit, by charging people to come into the pub and see it. Local opinion was outraged, the newspaper calling it utterly callous to all sense of decency. King was hanged, and no doubt there were those who would have liked to see Mrs Pullen Senior join him.

GUNFIGHT AT THE KINGSCLERE SALOON

In October 1944 an incident took place in the village of Kingsclere, just south of Newbury (and marginally in Hampshire, but who's arguing?). It was felt to pose such a serious threat to international (and race) relations that a future American president felt it necessary to intervene.

A US Army engineering unit arrived in the village, and was stationed at Sydmonton Court. On the night of 5 October, ten

African American soldiers decided to sneak out of camp and sample the fleshpots of Kingsclere. At the Swan Inn they were confronted by a group of Military Police, who ordered them back to their barracks: (a) because they had no passes to be out and (b) because they were improperly dressed in their working clothes, rather than their uniforms.

The ten returned to camp, but only to arm themselves with loaded M1 carbines. They returned to the village and toured the pubs until they found the MPs drinking in the Crown. They lay in wait for them in the churchyard opposite. When two of them, named Anderson and Brown, left the pub, they were met with a hail of gunfire. Brown escaped injury, but Anderson fled the scene, badly wounded, only to die in a nearby garden. The soldiers continued to fire on the pub, leaving two more people, including the landlady, Rose Napper, dead or dying. The American Military Police responded in force and, within forty-eight hours, all ten offenders were in custody.

The English authorities opened an inquest for Mrs Napper but were forced, under wartime emergency regulations, to abandon it almost immediately, having established only who she was and which part of her had been shot – that is, just enough evidence to allow her funeral to take place. Despite a British citizen having been shot on British soil, the British authorities were powerless to take any action against her murderers. The administration of justice to them was left entirely in the hands of the US Army.

Relations between the locals and the troops were already (according to some accounts) said to be delicate, with claims of theft, sexual assaults and other misdemeanours being levelled at the soldiers. The situation was sensitive enough for the head of the American forces, General Eisenhower, to send a personal message to the people of Kingsclere through their local newspaper, regretting:

> ... that this most unfortunate and regrettable affair, resulting in the death of a local resident, should have occurred and been caused by United States troops. He sincerely hoped that the effect of this occurrence would not tend to excite public opinion and tend to detract from the friendly good feeling and spirit of cooperation which existed between our two English-speaking nations.

> (*Newbury Weekly News* – 26 October 1944)

Nine of the guilty parties were given whole life prison sentences at their courts martial. The tenth was originally only charged with being absent without leave, for which he received a ten-year sentence, but his term was later increased in line with the others at a retrial. The rest of the unit was rapidly redeployed overseas. As for Private Anderson, his ghost is said to walk the Crown Inn to this day.

THE HUNGERFORD MASSACRE

In 1987 the small Berkshire town of Hungerford was the site of one of the worst cases of criminal violence involving firearms ever seen in the United Kingdom. Seventeen people, including the perpetrator, were killed and a further fifteen wounded.

Michael Ryan was a 27-year-old unemployed labourer and antiques dealer. He lived with his widowed mother, who worked as a dinner lady at the nearby primary school. People described their relationship as 'unhealthy' and said that she spoiled him – 'a mummy's boy' one headline called him, and another said he was 'more Bambi than Rambo'. He had an unhealthy obsession with guns. At the time of the massacre he was licensed to possess two shotguns, three pistols (two of them semi-automatic) and two semi-automatic rifles.

On 17 August, Ryan set out for the Savernake Forest, the boot of his car filled with weapons. Nobody knows his motive for the events that followed, for the two people who might have been able to throw some light on it – Ryan himself, and his mother – would be among the fatalities. In the forest, he came upon Sue Godfrey and her two children having a picnic, and shot her ten times in the back. He then returned to Hungerford, stopping on the way at a petrol station where he narrowly failed to shoot the cashier, only leaving when his gun ran out of ammunition.

Back in Hungerford, he returned home, loaded his car with survival gear, then shot the family dog, doused the house with petrol and set it alight. Two neighbours who came to see what the commotion was were shot dead. Ryan then set off walking through the streets of Hungerford, loaded with weapons and an ammunition belt and shooting more or less anyone he came across – including his doting mother, whom he met on her way back from doing the shopping. Eventually Ryan entered a house in Priory Road, shooting dead the elderly occupants, one of whom was in a wheelchair. He next made his way into the nearby (and empty) John of Gaunt Technology College, which he had attended as a pupil.

By now, armed police had the area surrounded. They had to be brought in from some 40 miles away, since Ryan could comfortably outgun any weapons the local police possessed. One of the policemen had a shouted conversation with Ryan, who seemed mainly concerned about how his mother was, claiming that her shooting had been a mistake. Then a final pistol shot was heard – Ryan had taken his own life. Some of his reported last words were 'Hungerford must be a bit of a mess. I wish I had stayed in bed.'

The home secretary commissioned a report into the events of the day, which led to the passing of the Firearms (Amendment) Act 1988. This banned the ownership of semi-automatic centre-fire rifles and restricted the use of shotguns with a capacity of more than three cartridges. This did not, however, prevent the Dunblane massacre of 1996 or the 2010 Cumbria shootings.

The massacre naturally attracted worldwide press attention, not all of it accurate. Some tried to claim that Ryan had had an obsession with the film character Rambo, who also specialised in mass executions (though it was unlikely that he had ever seen the film). The actor who played Rambo – Sylvester Stallone – was prompted to issue a statement to the effect that the values of Rambo were exactly the opposite of those of Michael Ryan. Medical experts tried posthumous diagnosis, but were reduced to suspicions – against which it would be difficult to argue – that Ryan was psychotic and schizophrenic.

HANGED, BUT NOT FOR MURDER

We tend to associate the supreme punishment – the death sentence – with the supreme crime – murder. But for much of recorded history, hanging was the sentence for a host of lesser offences, some of which we might today regard as relatively minor.

Taking Reading Gaol as an example, between 1800 and 1833 nineteen people were hanged for lesser offences. In 1802, the theft of two heifers from Mortimer Fair led Edward Painter to the gallows, leaving ten impoverished children to mourn his loss. The following year, Dennis Daley was found guilty of issuing a false cheque for £10 (in those days, cheques were handwritten on plain pieces of paper and easy to forge). The judge at his trial was apparently outraged by his action. He ruled that:

... the offence was one of such magnitude as never to be pardoned. In the case of forgery, death follows at the stroke of a pen.

Even the issuing of a single forged £1 note was enough to see John Newbank hanged in 1815. It seems he was anxious to advance his daughters' position in society and had rather fallen into debt doing so.

You also needed to be careful of the company you kept in those days. Thomas Cox of Tilehurst found himself facing the gallows after a rather drunken village fair had led to him committing bestiality in front of witnesses. Contemporary reports were understandably coy about the details of the offence, which was apparently not particularly uncommon in rural areas in the days when you had to make your own entertainment.

For some, the death penalty seems to have been an acceptable occupational hazard of their chosen profession. Charles White was a horse thief, described as being 'notorious in six counties'. He had attended the hanging of four of his sons for the same offence in 1812, at which he had apparently eaten a hearty meal and commented on the merits of each one as a horse thief as they went to meet their maker. It clearly had no deterrent effect on him, for he himself was hanged in 1814.

For some of those executed, it was simply a matter of luck that their crime was not one of murder. In 1828 the crowds in Reading were treated to the rare spectacle of a triple hanging. They were part of a gang of twelve poachers, whose activities on the Crutchley Park estate, near Sunninghill, were interrupted by two gamekeepers. The unfortunate pair were shot and left for dead, but survived the ordeal.

The careers of some of our local highwaymen are dealt with in chapter 7, but there were a number more who, having been executed, did not come back to trouble us:

Philip Stafford, born in about 1622 near Newbury, turned to highway robbery after his estates were confiscated following the Civil War. He robbed under the name 'Captain Stafford', mostly worked around Maidenhead Thicket, and was caught after robbing a farmer on the Reading Road. It is said that, on the day of his execution, he had a drink with the hangman on his way to the gallows, promising to pay on his way back.

William Davis had the highwayman stage name 'The Golden Farmer' and spent forty-five years leading a double life, as a God-fearing farmer by day and a highwayman by night (though he cannot have been out every night, since he also managed to father eighteen children). He was finally caught and hanged in Bagshot Heath at the age of 64, in 1690.

But the prize for a double life must go to Sir John Popham of Littlecote, near Hungerford. He had a ten-year career as a highwayman, before being persuaded by his wife to go straight. Not only did he go straight, he went straight to the top, becoming Lord Chief Justice, in which capacity he sent down many of his former accomplices.

The 'Wokingham Blacks' were a band, led by a farmer called Will Shorter, who combined highway robbery with blackmail, robbery, murder and all sorts of other unpleasantness. They were so called because they used to black their faces up to commit their crimes. So notorious were they that they provoked their own legislation (the Black Act 1723) making it an offence punishable by death to wear black faces with criminal intent (though how much of a deterrent the Act would be to already committed highwaymen and murderers is open to question).

Twenty-nine of them were eventually caught after a pitched battle with Grenadier Guards that same year, and four of them were hanged in chains. The membership of the group looked highly respectable, including as it did a clergyman, a farmer, two 'gentlemen' and assorted skilled tradesmen, and it lends credence to an alternative view, that they were not just a bunch of cut-throats but a group with a social and political purpose. This would argue that the powerful Whigs at this time were looking to monopolise the forests and were trying to drive the common people from it with restrictive regulations and exorbitant fees for everything. Under this theory, the Blacks directed their attacks on the big landowners and those agents who put their policies into practice.

But the most famous highwayman, who is alleged to have drunk at just about every old pub in the land, is Dick Turpin. He was not a local man, being born in Essex, but was said to have hideouts in many of the inns around Windsor Forest and Bagshot Heath. One, the Hind's Head, was said to have a secret tunnel large enough to

Dick Turpin

conceal both Turpin and his horse. Turpin was hanged at Tyburn in 1739.

One of the last highwaymen to be hanged for offences along the notorious Bath Road was George Wiggins, in 1820. His immediate crime had been the beating up and robbing of one James Leach, near Thatcham. Though only 22 years old, his comprehensive confession also included eleven highway robberies, eight burglaries and over forty thefts.

MORE MAD THAN BAD

For many years mental illness was little understood and its victims harshly treated. Some of the inmates of London's Bethlem Hospital (also known as 'Bedlam'), founded in 1247, were kept permanently chained, and until 1770 their antics provided a ghoulish entertainment for casual visitors.

More humane regimes were gradually established during the reign of Queen Victoria, culminating in the 1863 opening of Broadmoor, near Crowthorne. This started out as the Broadmoor Criminal Lunatic Asylum, but is now described as a high security mental hospital. The names reflect the tensions it has wrestled with throughout its existence, between the therapeutic treatment of sick people and the incarceration of some of society's most dangerous individuals. Its two rings of 17ft walls and the regularly tested escape alarms of the modern establishment make it look from the outside like a prison, but its aim from the start has been to try and nurse its inmates back to health. At first, in the days before anti-psychotic drugs, they had little to offer but kindness and comfort.

Their very first patient was a woman convicted of infanticide, whom modern medicine might well regard as being a victim of post-natal depression and/or congenital syphilis. Other inmates have included alcoholics, narcissists, the victims of grief and obsessive practitioners of what the Victorians sometimes called 'the solitary vice'.

But it has also housed some very dangerous people. These have included not one but two of the men suspected of being Jack the

Broadmoor Criminal Lunatic Asylum, 1906

Ripper – the wife murderer James Kelly, and Thomas Cutbush, after whose incarceration the Ripper murderers mysteriously stopped. Broadmoor also currently houses Jack's undisputed modern counterpart, Peter Sutcliffe, the Yorkshire Ripper. There was the gangster Ronnie Kray, his henchman, Frank 'the Mad Axeman' Mitchell and the self-styled Charles Bronson. The rare distinction of being refused admission to Broadmoor went to Moors murderer Ian Brady, after doctors could find no shred of humanity in him that might form a basis for treatment.

The hospital's policy of rehabilitation has also led to occasional problems. In 1951, lax security allowed convicted child murderer John Straffen to slip out and commit another. In 1962, Graham Young was confined there after fatally poisoning his stepmother at the age of 14 – mainly because he was too young to go to a secure prison. After nine years' treatment he was deemed to be no longer a danger. He was let out and inexplicably got a job in a photographic laboratory, where he was surrounded by dangerous chemicals (Broadmoor was not allowed to tell prospective employers about former inmates' funny little ways). It was not long before seventy of the local community went down with mystery illnesses, two of them dying. It did not take long to track down the guilty party and Young spent the rest of his days behind maximum security bars at Parkhurst Prison.

One of Broadmoor's more interesting inmates was a man who might stake a claim as Berkshire's greatest artist – in that he did much of his work whilst a patient at Broadmoor. Richard Dadd was an award-winning graduate of the Royal Academy, but it was during a trip through Egypt that he started becoming delusional and violent, believing himself to be the servant of the Egyptian god Osiris. In 1843, Osiris persuaded him that his father was the devil in disguise and Richard duly stabbed him to death. Thereafter he resided first at Bethlem and, after its opening, at Broadmoor, where he continued to paint until his death in 1886. Today, collectors will pay fortunes for his work, though their quaint subject matter – fairies and other supernatural topics – sometimes sit oddly with his violent tendencies.

4

SPORTING BERKSHIRE

In this chapter we look at some of the favourite sporting activities in Berkshire, some of which have a national or international reputation (and a few of which definitely do not). Before you ask, we will not be visiting the polo at Smith's Lawn in Windsor Great Park, or the Eton Wall Game – there is quite enough aristocratic patronage of the mainstream sports we are investigating. To start with:

FOOTBALL AND THE ROYALS

Berkshire's leading football club are nicknamed the 'Royals', and with good reason. It turns out that the lady in line to become the Queen of England – the Duchess of Cambridge, and a Berkshire girl – is a Reading supporter. Fellow fans may have seen her at half time down at the Madejski Stadium, eating pies.

One of the earliest references to football also came from a royal source. In an edict, King Edward I (reigned 1272–1307) complained that the skill in shooting with arrows was almost totally laid aside for the purpose of useless and unlawful games, among which he numbered football. Local people were supposed to practice archery at their local butts in anticipation of being called up in the event of war (St Mary's Butts was Reading's practice range), but many locals preferred to kick a ball about.

The first record of a football match in Berkshire dates from 1598, when two parishes put out sides of unlimited numbers for a match at North Moreton, near Didcot. The respective parish church doors served as goals. The rules appear to have been fairly uninhibited. One participant, known as 'Ould Gunter', carried a dagger throughout the match, with which he murdered two of the opposition, Richard and John Gregorie. Marking your opponents really meant something in those days. What was particularly striking was that Gunter was

apparently the local parish priest, and there was no indication that he even got so much as a red card, let alone tried for murder.

Today we have sports development officers, but in 1628 it seems the authorities in Reading had quite the opposite. When two officials saw a group of soldiers playing football on the open space known as 'the Forbury' they attempted to confiscate the ball, 'which caused much trouble to the constables and officers and danger and hurt to many others'.

It was the nineteenth century before the rules of football were properly formalised (at Cambridge University in 1848), though it was scarcely football as we know it. There was a tape for a crossbar, one handed throw-ins taken by whoever got to the ball first, and ends were changed after each goal on a pitch up to 200 yards long. Passing was almost unknown, and individual players would try and dribble the ball into the net, as their team mates barged aside any opponent who got in the way.

A number of northern sides had been formed by 1871 (the year the FA Cup was established) when a meeting was called at Reading's old Bridge Street rooms in February. It was decided to form a Reading Football Club, thus making the Royals the oldest current League club south of the River Trent (albeit that they did not join the League until 1920). The club led a nomadic existence in their early years, playing at King's Meadow, Reading cricket ground, Coley Park and Caversham Cricket Club (the latter site only accessible by boat). In 1895 a local property developer, Edwin Jesse, offered the club a cheap deal on 4 acres of former gravel pit in West Reading. This became Elm Park, their home until 1998. The first match was abandoned due to flooding, a portent of the drainage difficulties they would experience for the next thirty years.

The club went professional in 1895, and became a founder member of the new Division 3 in 1920 (for younger readers, this is what we now call League One), and over the years has enjoyed long periods in the second tier (Championship), as well as two brief spells in the Premier League. They moved to their current stadium, nicknamed the 'Mad Stad', in 1998.

Two of the club's high and low points came in the FA Cup. In 1894, Reading (still then an amateur team) drew recent League champions, Preston North End, away. The opposition were known (with good reason) as the 'Invincibles' and, to make matters worse, they played on a pitch resembling the Somme battlefield, in a keening gale. The Reading team, playing in smooth-soled footwear, could barely stay on their feet, while the cunning northerners had studded boots which were black-leaded to throw off the mud. Reading were beaten 18–0, which is thought to be the worst defeat ever inflicted on any of the current Football League clubs. Their FA Cup highlight was in 1927, when they got to the semi-finals – ninety minutes from Wembley. Unfortunately, they were beaten 3–0 by Cardiff, who went on to take the Cup out of England for the first (and so far last) time.

DAYS AT THE RACES

Berkshire boasts no less than three leading horse racing tracks, including one which is considered to be among the greatest racing venues in the world:

Ascot

This is one of Britain's major racecourses, and is home to nine of the United Kingdom's thirty-two top flight Group 1 races. It is just 6 miles from Windsor Castle and is owned by the Crown Estate. Founded by Queen Anne in 1711, the site has been protected since 1813 by an Act of Parliament, to ensure it remains a racecourse for all time.

Since 1913 it has been run by a body set up by another Act of Parliament, the Ascot Authority, overseen by an appointee of the monarch. Royal patronage over the years has not always brought forward the most shining examples of monarchy. The event went into something of a hiatus following Anne's death in 1714, but was revived in the 1740s by George II's third son, William, the Duke of Cumberland. His main claim to historical fame was as the 'Butcher of Culloden', for his brutal repression of the Jacobite rebellion of 1745. Its other great champion, who did much to make it an elite social event, was the future George IV, Prince Regent from 1811, a notorious gambler, womaniser and glutton. He introduced the idea of a 'Royal Enclosure' and of the royal procession to the meeting.

The first permanent building was erected in 1794, seating 1,650 people. It was replaced in 1839 by a stand costing £10,000. This can be compared to the redevelopment of 2006, which cost £185 million and was roundly condemned for having too much of its space given over to restaurants, bars and corporate hospitality, and not enough for actually watching horse racing. This forced the organisers to spend a further £10 million, but it still left the ordinary racegoer with less viewing space than they had before the redevelopment.

Just in case anyone thinks it still has anything to do with horse racing, consider the arrangements for the most prestigious meeting of the year, Royal Ascot. The holy of holies for this event is the aforementioned Royal Enclosure, and to call it exclusive barely does it justice. Newcomers have to be recommended for admission by someone who has been a regular attendee of the enclosure for at least four years. Even regular attendees have to be invited to apply for a badge each year by a member of the Royal Household. There is also a strict dress code. For ladies, a day dress and hat is de rigueur, and the rules also lay down what pieces of bare flesh they are allowed to display. Anything involving shoulders, midriffs or upper legs will get them cast into outer darkness, badge or not. Men have to wear black or grey morning dress and top hat.

Press coverage of the people attending and their attire comfortably exceeds that of the racing (for which, incidentally, the prize money now tops £5 million). The event attracts some 300,000 visitors each year, making it Europe's largest race meeting – or fashion show.

Windsor

This venue has two contrasting names – 'Royal Windsor' and 'the People's Course'. The first formal race meetings took place here in 1866, though its informal links to racing go back to the time of Henry VIII, and Charles II used to hold race meetings at Datchet Mead. The current course is a figure of eight, located on an island in the middle of the Thames, and there is at least one recorded case of a horse going out of control and ending up in the river.

In 1926, Winston Churchill proposed the introduction of a betting levy and the bookmakers at Windsor rebelled by refusing to accept bets. This threat to bring the country to its knees proved too much for the government, who quickly withdrew the proposed levy. This appears to be the course's one claim to historical fame.

The more exclusive parts of the course also have a dress code, but after the Royal Enclosure at Ascot it sounds positively bohemian. Men are barred from wearing collarless shirts or T-shirts, sportswear, shorts, trainers or ripped or frayed jeans. For the ladies it appears to be absolutely no holds barred, beyond 'smart'. Fancy dress is not permitted in the Club Enclosure.

Newbury

Horse racing has been popular in the Newbury area since the time of Charles II. In the days before the Enclosure Acts many towns and villages had their own local race meetings, and one of the objections to enclosure was the loss of these social events. From 1740, race meetings were held at Wash Common and over the parkland of Sandford Priory. These events were often linked to the stationing of troops in camps on the common.

Enborne Heath staged its own race meetings from 1805 onwards. The Corporation of Newbury used to present a silver cup, valued at £50, to each meeting and, in 1815, a gold cup worth 100 guineas was added to the prizes. This race week became an excuse for a general festival in the town, with celebrations being held in the main hotels and inns, and a theatrical cast being brought down from London to perform for the visitors.

But Newbury racecourse itself has a much more recent origin. A horse trainer named John Porter had been trying unsuccessfully for a few years to get the Jockey Club to license a race meeting at Newbury, when he chanced to meet one of the owners for whom he trained, in Newmarket High Street. This meeting was decisive, for that owner was King Edward VII, and (according to some accounts) he cut through the red tape by simply licensing the meeting by royal

decree. A limited company was set up to fund the development of the course and the first meeting was held on 26 September 1905, making it the nation's second youngest racecourse. Porter himself only ever enjoyed one winner at Newbury, since he retired from racing at the end of the 1905 season.

One of the facilities planned from the outset was the course's own dedicated railway station, and it is thought that this played no small part in the course's subsequent success. However, the railway link was less helpful to it during the war years. During the First World War it was turned into a German Prisoner of War camp. From 1942, the racecourse was handed over to the American Army, who used it as a huge railway marshalling yard (see chapter 12). Racing was not resumed until 1949.

AND SOME FORGOTTEN RACE MEETINGS

Abingdon had a racecourse at Culham Heath from 1733. It continued until 1875, when the Clerk of the Course died and nobody could be found to take in his duties.

Reading Races were run between 1747 and 1873. They took place at Bulmershe Heath until 1813, when Bulmershe was enclosed, and thereafter at King's Meadow.

There is also a record of Maidenhead Races being held at Maidenhead Thicket in 1787, attended by the Royal Family.

HENLEY ROYAL REGATTA

Here we have yet another royal sporting event associated with the county and, before anybody writes to complain that Henley is not in Berkshire, my reasoning is that the racing takes place (and most spectators gather) on the Berkshire side of the Thames.

In 1839, a meeting was held in Henley, at which one Captain Edmund Gardiner called for a regatta 'under judicious and respectable management' that would be 'a source of amusement and gratification to the neighbourhood'. Thus began the Henley Regatta, which has been held every year since (bar the two world wars). It began mainly as a fairground and other amusements, but the rowing soon came to dominate the proceedings, which extended from one afternoon in 1839 to the current five days (plus qualifying races in the preceding weeks).

It was not the first boat race of note to be conducted along this stretch of the Thames. The first Oxford and Cambridge boat race was run between Hambleden Lock and Henley Bridge in 1829.

It is 'royal' because, from 1851 Prince Albert became its patron and, since his death, every reigning monarch has agreed to do likewise. It was established long before any national or international bodies governing rowing existed, and so follows its own, sometimes quirky, rules. For example, the length of the course (which is strictly observed) is 1 mile 550 yards, 112m longer than the current international standard of 2,000m. It is also held on a flowing river, rather than the still waters of a rowing lake. This caused considerable problems of its own for many years. The old course (used until 1885) had a left-hand bend, which favoured the Berkshire side (both in terms of distance to be covered and currents). The course was then changed, but this was found to favour the other side, in terms of shelter from unfavourable winds. This was again changed from 1922 and, with a good deal of excavation, a straight and even-handed course was finally arrived at.

Since 1884 it has been run by a self-elected body of stewards, generally ex-rowers. The regatta is unusual, if not unique, among major sporting events in that the £3 million it takes to stage it each year is found without sponsorship or subsidy. About three-quarters of it comes from subscriptions from the stewards' enclosure. Membership of the enclosure is limited to about 6,500 and there is a long waiting list of about 900, with priority being given to former competitors.

Among their more idiosyncratic rules was their strict amateurism. A detailed definition of 'amateur' was provided in 1879, which would be quaint, were it not so elitist. Among those who were excluded were anyone:

> ... who has ever taught, pursued or assisted in the practice of athletic exercises of any kind as a means of gaining a livelihood;
> ... who has been in or about boats for money or wages;
> ... who has been by trade or employment a mechanic, artisan or labourer.

For good measure, in 1886 they also debarred any person 'engaged in any menial activity'. Through these rules, in 1920 they excluded

future Olympic champion John B. Kelly Senior, who had worked as a 'menial' bricklayer and (in 1906) the Vesper Boat Club, who had rendered themselves 'professional' by paying for their travelling expenses to Henley by means of a public subscription.

The regatta's amateurism really collided with the twentieth century in 1936, when the Australian Olympic crew were debarred, on the grounds that they were policemen (deemed by the stewards to be a menial occupation). The row that this caused led to the deletion of the exclusions relating to manual work and menial activity. Amateurism was finally abandoned in 1998.

The stewards were equally forward looking when it came to their dealings with women competitors. Women coxes were allowed from 1975, but female rowers were excluded, partly on the grounds that the stewards thought the 2,112m course would be too much for their poor little arms (international women's events were then run over 1,000m). Kingston Rowing Club tried to force the issue in 1978 by entering two well-known women internationals under their maiden names and just an initial for their Christian names. But it would be 1993 before women's events found a permanent place in the programme (by which time, the international standard for women's races had been raised to 2,000m).

Being 'royal', the event became a must for those who moved in exalted circles – hence, no doubt, the waiting list for the Stewards' Enclosure. Naturally enough, the enclosure had its own dress code, and readers who have got this far in the chapter will by now be a connoisseur of them. Gentlemen will require a lounge suit, blazer and flannels, or evening dress and a tie. Ladies' dresses must cover their knees and they are 'encouraged' to wear a hat. And, just in case anyone should be tempted to try and contact the twenty-first century from inside the enclosure, mobile phone use there is prohibited.

CRICKET

Berkshire may not be a major force in cricket, but it can claim a couple of footnotes in the history of the game. Reading was the birthplace of not just two England cricket captains, but two Ashes-winning England cricket captains, in A.P.F. Chapman (1928–29) and Peter May (1956). The town also gave us England batsman Ken Barrington and the Bedser twins, Alec and Eric (Surrey and, in Alec's case, England, stalwarts).

There seems to be some doubt as to when cricket was first played in, or by, Berkshire. One source claims it was a match against the Marylebone Cricket Club in 1793, played at the MCC's home ground, Lords. Among the MCC side was a Mr Thomas Lord, after whom the famous ground was named. A wager of 500 guineas was staked on the game, which MCC lost.

Another claim to antiquity was a match against Surrey in 1769, and a third cites one in 1751, but cricket was being played in neighbouring Surrey in 1550 and it is likely to have reached Berkshire (however informally) sometime in the sixteenth century.

Thomas Waymark, generally regarded as the game's first great all-rounder, was a Berkshire resident and was recorded as playing for Berkshire sides in the 1740s. The picture is somewhat complicated by the fact that Maidenhead's Oldfield club (they played at the Old

Field, Bray) was for a long time the de facto county side. The county side (however defined) was certainly among the nation's leading teams in the 1790s and in 1794 was actually listed as the nation's strongest county side. But soon afterwards, following a defeat by the MCC in 1795, the side mysteriously disappeared from the first class schedules. The current Berkshire County Cricket Club was formed in 1895, but has always been one of the minor counties.

'ROYAL' PUGILISM AND RELATED VIOLENCE

Bare-knuckle boxing, or pugilism, was a hugely popular sport in the eighteenth and early nineteenth centuries. To us it may seem brutal and bloodthirsty, but to its aficionados at the time it was regarded as humane, fair, chivalrous and a symbol of national courage of which Britain could be proud.

Berkshire, being close to London, was a favourite venue, and its long county boundaries also worked for the promoters. For the sport was not strictly legal, and a favourite ploy was to hold the event at a venue close to a county boundary. That way, if the authorities looked like breaking up a fight, the participants could swiftly disappear across the county boundary, and finish the event before the neighbouring authorities got wind of their presence.

Legal or not, the 'sport' enjoyed avid support in the highest circles. Many of the Royal Family were enthusiasts and, when the police broke up one bout, the celebrities who had to be hurriedly smuggled out included the Prince of Wales, Prime Minister Palmerston and authors Charles Dickens and William Thackeray.

In the late eighteenth century the George Inn at Wargrave was the home of an entire 'stable' (if that is the right word) of the nation's leading pugilists, maintained at the expense of the Earl of Barrymore, who was himself a keen fighter. He once got one of his most successful protégés to dress up as a vicar, and took him down to London's Vauxhall Pleasure Gardens, where he dispensed sound thrashings to some no-doubt-surprised fairground pugilists. Barrymore was also one of those who bet prodigious sums on the outcome of fights. He won £25,000 when his 11 stone protégé beat a bargee weighing 16 stone, and William Hazlitt tells of a total of £200,000 being staked on one Berkshire fight he attended. Barrymore was also noted for lavish theatrical productions and fancy dress parties, and it will come as no surprise that he went bankrupt shortly before his death in 1793.

The railways made access to events easier and, to make it more difficult for the authorities to gain advance knowledge of the venue, the railways were known to issue tickets marked 'to nowhere'. One event in 1842 was held in the railway yard at Twyford station, suggesting even closer connivance between the railway company and the promoter.

The fights – and individual rounds – were of indeterminate length. Rounds ended when one of the protagonists was knocked down and fights could end with the loser being carried insensible from the ring or being 'almost unrecognisable as a human being'. Hazlitt, again, describes the face of one pugilist, a dozen or so rounds into a bout he saw at Hungerford:

His face was like a human skull, a death's head, spouting blood. The eyes were filled with blood, the nose streamed with blood, the mouth gaped blood.

Even in this state, he still managed to continue the contest for several more rounds. It was said of this particular fighter, known as the 'Gas Man', that if his hands were cut off, he would continue to fight with the stumps, and it was by no means unknown for fighters to die of their wounds. One fight went on for 180 rounds, lasting three and a half hours, before being declared a draw.

But it was not just the contest itself that led the authorities to oppose these events. The unruly behaviour of the crowds also posed a threat to public order. At one bout, fans of one of the fighters threatened to lynch the unfortunate referee if he did not award the fight to their man. After a particularly nasty riot at Paddington in 1863, pressure increased for the sport to be cleaned up or effectively banned. The Marquis of Queensbury rules, by which modern boxing is governed, were approved by Parliament in 1865 and the Regulation of Railways Act 1868 made it an offence for railway companies to run pugilism specials, and set up a system of rewards for anyone reporting a forthcoming event to the authorities.

MORE BRUTALITY: CUDGEL PLAY, CUT-LEGS, KICK-SHINS AND BULL-BAITING

Cudgel play was a native Berkshire sport in the nineteenth century. The combatants were issued with cudgels and the object of the game was to strike the opponent's head and draw blood, at which point the crowd would shout 'a head' and a winner declared.

Weirder still, were two games which the *Victoria History of Berkshire* thought were unique to the county. This introduction comes from the 1906 volume of the *History*:

> Every race has its peculiarity, and where the negro is tenderest, the Berkshire man is toughest – in his shins. As a backdrop at cricket he prefers to stop the fastest balls with his shins, rather than with his hands, and will keep on all day without apparent inconvenience.

It seems there were two versions of the game. With 'cut-legs', two carters would stand apart and lash each other's shins with their long whips until one cried 'hold' and paid for the drinks. 'Kick-shins' involved two yokels grasping each other by the collar and then kicking each other in the shins with their hob-nail boots until one yielded. Unsurprisingly, these sports were not without risk:

> There was living in the Lambourn Valley about forty years ago a man who was considered the champion of the countryside, and his shins were knotted and bent and twisted in the most remarkable manner, as the result of his numerous encounters.

Thankfully, all of these games had died out by the start of the twentieth century.

Wokingham's claim to sporting fame seems to be that it was once celebrated for its bull-baiting. In 1661 one George Staverton made a bequest to pay for two bulls to be baited in the Market Place each St Thomas' Day. The bulls were first paraded around the town, then attached to a post in the Market Place by about 5 yards of chain. The object of the preliminaries was to get the bull fighting mad and, if the tumult of the parade did not have the desired effect, the organisers would blow pepper up the beast's nostrils. A series of bulldogs were then released to attack the bull. The objective was for the dog to seize the bull by its nose and pull its head down, which was called 'pinning the bull'.

In one bout witnessed by a local historian, the first dog to attack was impaled on the bull's horns and hurled high into the air. Another dog went to entirely the wrong end of the bull, seizing what our correspondent describes as 'a tender part'. In its agony, the bull broke its chain and ran amok through the streets. Fatalities were not unknown among the crowds attending these events. Characteristically, the event ended with the crowd, many of whom had been quarrelling throughout the day, starting a mass brawl. Strange as it may seem, bull-baiting actually once had a purpose (beyond gratifying sadists) in that it was believed to improve the taste of the beast's meat.

Invariably the bull, once it had been baited enough, was slaughtered and its meat and leather distributed to the poor. This barbarous activity was outlawed by the Corporation in 1821, though the practice of slaughtering bulls (unbaited) and distributing their meat to the poor continued. Bull-baiting was outlawed by Parliament in the Cruelty to Animals Act 1835.

For good measure, the Bull Inn at Bracknell was also said to be a noted bull-baiting venue, one which Henry VIII used to visit.

Finally, lest it be thought that Royal Windsor is excluded from this catalogue of cruelty, the *London Gazette* of 2 July 1685 carried an advertisement promising: '... a great match of cock-fighting at Windsor between two persons of quality, which continues for that whole week'.

5

BERKSHIRE PEOPLE

In this chapter I have listed some of the famous people with links to Berkshire – either they were born or died there, were educated there or lived in the county for a significant period in their lives. I have had to make some exceptions. The main one was to exclude people whose only link with the county was being educated at Eton; otherwise it would be a catalogue of half of the ruling elites of the past several centuries.

KINGS, QUEENS AND ASSORTED ROYALTY (INCLUDING PEOPLE WITH LINKS TO ROYALTY)

A number of our monarchs have a rather permanent association with Berkshire, by virtue of being buried there. Most are at Windsor Castle:

Henry VI (1421–71) was born at Windsor. He was originally buried at Chertsey Abbey, but reinterred at Windsor in 1485.

Edward IV (1442–83)
Henry VIII (1491–1547)
Charles I (1600–49)
George III (1738–1820)
George IV (1762–1830)
William IV (1765–1837)
Edward VII (1841–1910)
George V (1864–1936)
George VI (1895–1952)

In addition, **Queen Victoria** (1819–1901) is buried at Frogmore in Windsor Great Park and **Edward VIII** (1894–1972) in the Royal Cemetery in Windsor Great Park.

Henry I (1068–1135) is buried somewhere in the ruins of the Reading Abbey that he founded.

Edward III (1312–77) went against the standard royal practice, by being born at Windsor but buried in Westminster Abbey.

Alfred the Great (AD 849–899) was born in what is now Wantage. He was King of Wessex between 871 and 899.

William Marshal (1147–1219) owned the estate at Caversham Park, Reading, where he spent the last months of his life and from where he effectively ran the country as regent, during the minority of King Henry III.

Alfred the Great

King Henry VIII

Louis Mountbatten (1900–79) was born at Frogmore House, Windsor. He was uncle to Prince Philip, second cousin (once removed) to the Queen and was variously (amongst other roles) First Sea Lord, Chief of the Defence Staff and Viceroy of India.

Catherine of Aragon (1485–1536) stayed at Easthampstead House, Bracknell, while the details of her divorce from Henry VIII were being arranged.

Turning to living royalty, **Prince William** (1982–) was educated at Ludgrove School near Wokingham, Eton and the Royal Military Academy, Sandhurst. His brother, **Prince Harry** (1984–) attended the same three establishments. **Katherine, Duchess of Cambridge** (1982–) was born at the Royal Berkshire Hospital, Reading and raised at Chapel Row, near Newbury. She attended St Andrews School, Pangbourne.

PRIME MINISTERS AND POLITICIANS

Henry Addington (1757–1844) lived for many years at Bulmershe Court, and donated the land for the Royal Berkshire Hospital, Reading. He was prime minister (1801–04) and the first Viscount Sidmouth.

David Cameron (1966–) was brought up in Peasemore and educated at Heatherdown Preparatory School, Winkfield, and Eton. Prime minister from 2010.

Michael Foot (1913–2010) was educated at Leighton Park School, Reading. He was an MP, and Leader of the Labour Party in opposition.

Rufus Isaacs (1860–1935) lived at Foxhill House, Earley. He was a barrister, Lord Chief Justice, foreign secretary, Viceroy of India and the first Viscount Reading.

Francis Maude (1953–) was born in Abingdon (then in Berkshire), and was educated at Abingdon School. A Conservative MP, minister and one-time chairman of the Conservative Party.

CHURCHMEN

Hugh Cook Faringdon (died 1539) was born in Faringdon, when it was part of Berkshire. Abbot of Reading 1520–39. Executed at Reading as a consequence of the dissolution of the monasteries. Declared a saint by the Roman Catholic Church in 1895.

William Laud (1573–1645) was born in Reading. Archbishop of Canterbury 1633–40. Impeached by Parliament during the Civil War and executed for treason.

Cormac Murphy-O'Connor (1932–) was born in Reading and educated at Presentation College. Archbishop of Westminster and head of the Roman Catholic Church in England and Wales (2000–09).

Edmund Rich (1180–1240) was born in Abingdon. Archbishop of Canterbury 1233–40, canonised as Saint Edmund of Abingdon in 1247. His sisters Alice and Margaret were also canonised.

AUTHORS

Jane Austen (1775–1817) studied at the Abbey School, Reading, from 1785.

John Betjeman (1906–84) lived in Wantage (then in Berkshire) 1951–72. Poet, (Poet Laureate 1972–84), writer and campaigner for Victorian architecture.

Michael Bond (1926–) was born in Newbury, and raised in Reading. Almost killed in the 1943 air raid on Reading. Author of the Paddington Bear books.

Robert Bridges (1844–1930) educated at Eton and lived at Yattendon for twenty-two years. Poet (Poet Laureate from 1913 until 1930).

Agatha Christie (1890–1976) lived for periods at Sunningdale and at Wallingford (formerly part of Berkshire), where she died.

D.H. Lawrence (1885–1930) and his wife lived at Hermitage between 1917 and 1919, and rented a cottage in Pangbourne in 1919. They suffered police harassment during their stay, due to his wife Frieda being a German and, moreover, a cousin of the German First World War air ace, Manfred von Richthofen.

Alexander Pope (1688–1744) lived at Binfield from the age of 12. His father made a fortune as a linen draper and bought an imposing country house in the village. Pope's Meadow is named after him. Among his early compositions was one called 'Windsor Forest'. Poet.

Percy Bysshe Shelley (1792–1822) spent part of his youth living in the Bracknell area. During his time there he wrote 'Queen Mab'. He once rowed across a pond in Braybrook in an old bath tub, for a bet. There used to be a 'Shelley's Cottage' in Easthampstead. Poet.

Percy Bysshe Shelley

Oscar Wilde

Oscar Wilde (1854–1900) was imprisoned 1895–97 for homosexual offences, part of which was spent in Reading Gaol. The experience was the inspiration for his works 'De Profundis' and 'The Ballad of Reading Gaol'. Author, playwright, wit.

ARTISTS

Richard Dadd (1817–86) was a resident of Broadmoor 1863–86. Painter and murderer.

Stanley Spencer (1891–1959) was born and lived in Cookham, and died at Cliveden. Painter.

ACTORS, COMEDIANS, ENTERTAINERS

Kenneth Branagh (1960–) was born in Northern Ireland but lived in Reading from the age of 9 'to escape the troubles'. Educated at Whiteknights Primary School and the Meadway School. Actor and film director.

Jimmy Carr (1972–) grew up in Slough. Attended Farnham Common School and Burnham Grammar School. Comedian, television host and actor.

Alma Cogan (1932–66) was educated at St Joseph's Convent, Reading. Popular singer.

Ricky Gervais (1961–) was born and raised in Whitley, Reading. Attended Whitley Park and Ashmead schools. Comedian, actor, director, musician, writer, etc.

Elton John (1947–) has his main residence at Old Windsor. Singer-songwriter.

Christopher Lee (1922–) was educated at Wellington College. Actor.

Humphrey Lyttelton (1921–2008) was born in Eton (his father was a house master at the college). Attended Sunningdale School and Eton. Jazz musician and radio presenter.

Robert Morley (1908–92) was educated at Wellington College and lived for much of his life at Crazies Hill, near Maidenhead. Died at Wargrave. Oscar-nominated actor.

Dennis Price (1915–73) was born in Twyford and attended Copthorne Preparatory School. Actor.

Terence Rattigan (1911–77) lived at Sonning for several years after the Second World War. Playwright.

Kate Winslet (1975–) was born in Reading. Studied drama from the age of 11 at the Redroofs Theatre School, Maidenhead. Actress, singer.

SPORTSMEN

Ken Barrington (1930–81) was born in Reading. Attended Wilson Primary School and Katesgrove Secondary School. England cricketer.

Alec (1918–2010) and **Eric** (1918–2006) **Bedser** were born in Reading. Twin brothers and cricketers. Alec was reckoned to be one of the finest English players of the twentieth century and Eric played for Surrey for twenty-three years.

A.P.F. (Percy) Chapman (1900–61) was born in Reading. England cricket captain.

Peter May (1929–94) was born in Reading. England cricket captain.

Peter Osgood (1947–2006) was born in Windsor. Chelsea and England footballer.

Lester Piggot (1935–) was born in Wantage (when part of Berkshire). Jockey.

Theo Walcott (1989–) grew up in Compton and attended Compton C of E Primary School and the Downs School. Arsenal and England footballer.

FILM PEOPLE

John (1913–85) and **Roy** (1913–2001) **Boulting** were born at Bray and educated at Reading School. John died at Sunningdale. Film producers, directors and screenwriters.

David Lean (1908–91) was educated at Leighton Park School, Reading. Film director and producer.

Sam Mendes (1965–) was born in Reading. Film and stage director.

FLYING PEOPLE

Sydney Camm (1893–1966) was born and grew up in Windsor. Educated at the Royal Free School, Windsor. Aircraft designer, whose work included the Hawker Hurricane, the Hawker Hunter and the Harrier jump jet.

W.E. Johns (1893–1968) first learned to fly at the military flying school at Coley Park, Reading, in 1917. Author of the Biggles books.

Charles Portal (1893–1971) was born in Hungerford. Chief of Air Staff during the Second World War. Later became the first Viscount Portal of Hungerford.

OTHER NOTABLES

William Henry Fox Talbot (1800–77), inventor of the modern photographic process, set up his first photographic processing establishment in Reading.

William Penn (1644–1718) died at Ruscombe, near Twyford. Real estate entrepreneur, philosopher, early Quaker and founder of Pennsylvania.

John Soane (1753–1837) was born in Goring-on-Thames and privately educated in Reading. Architect, whose works included the Bank of England.

Jethro Tull (1674–1741) was born in Basildon and grew up in Bradfield. Inventor of the horse drawn seed drill and other agricultural advances.

6

BERKSHIRE CASTLES, ABBEYS AND STATELY HOMES

In this chapter we look at the story behind some of Berkshire's greatest monuments (or in some cases what is left of them).

WINDSOR CASTLE

Windsor is the largest inhabited castle in the world, and a stately home beyond the dreams of the richest Russian oligarch. Windsor Castle has over 1,000 years of history, if you include the Saxon palace at nearby Old Windsor. This preceded and, for some time, overlapped with the present structure, and Edward the Confessor is recorded as having been in residence there in 1061. The Saxon kings located their palace there, in the ninth century or earlier, because of the transport links provided by the River Thames and the hunting in nearby Windsor Forest (not, as one American tourist thought, for its proximity to Heathrow Airport!).

But who built Windsor Castle? The answer is extremely complicated.

When William the Conqueror invaded, one of the means by which he secured his new territory was by building a ring of forts around London, each of them about a day's march away. Windsor was an obvious candidate for such a fort. The castle site stood on a 100ft cliff of chalk offering natural protection on three sides. The chalk geology offered a secure source of pure water and, in addition to the transport links by river, it lay on strategic roads between the capital and the upper Thames and Kennet valleys. The area (and its hunting) was also known to William through his association with Old Windsor. In about 1070, William commissioned a castle,

arranged in three wards and surrounded by ditches and ramparts. At its centre, on an artificial mound nearly 50ft high, stood a wooden fortress, protected by a deep ditch. The castle site was already something like its present size – over 500 yards from one end to the other and covering some 13 acres. But, whatever its merits as a military structure, it was not yet deemed to be habitable for royalty. The Royal Court would not assemble there until 1110.

Henry II (reigned 1154–89) commissioned the first stone buildings – including royal lodgings, the Round Tower and stone outer walls on every side, except the steep western flank.

Henry III (reigned 1216–72) started building a chapel, one wall of which survives in the Dean's Cloister. Between 1220 and 1230 he also added the west wall with its semi-circular towers. In the north-west corner stood the Curfew Tower, with walls up to 13ft thick.

Edward III (reigned 1327–77) who was born in the castle, added many adornments to it and also founded the Order of the Garter there. The origins of the Order seem to date back to what sounds like a lavish party, thrown in the castle in 1344:

> At the costly banquets were the most alluring of drinks in plenty, enough and to spare. The lords and ladies failed not to dance, mingling kisses with embraces ... The joy was unspeakable, the comfort inestimable, the pleasure without murmuring, the hilarity without care.

This bun fight, built around the excuse of a Round Table meeting of the great and the good, was apparently where the idea of the Order originated (it was finally founded in 1348).

Edward IV's (reigned 1461–83) main contribution to the castle, as we know it, was to start the building of St George's Chapel in 1475. However, it was not finished until 1528, well into the reign of Henry VIII (reigned 1509–47). Henry's best known contribution was the main entrance gateway; the pomegranate badge on it is that of his first wife, Catherine of Aragon. Prior to this, Henry VII (reigned 1485–1509) had set in motion the rebuilding of the old castle chapel, partly to provide a burial place for himself and Henry VI. However, he died before it was completed and Cardinal Wolsey had it finished to serve as a grand tomb for himself. He fell from grace in 1529 and Henry VIII took it back, thinking that he would be buried there, but he ended up in St George's Chapel and this tomb was left in mothballs for the next 100 years. The ornate metalwork commissioned by Wolsey was finally sold for £600 in 1646, and the marble base went to St Paul's in 1808, to cover Nelson's grave.

Charles I's (reigned 1625–49) main impact on the castle was in getting Prince Rupert to bombard it with cannon during its occupation by Parliamentary forces. This half-hearted attempt to capture it did more damage to the town than it did to the castle itself.

Under the Commonwealth, shortage of money almost forced the government of the day to sell off the castle, along with other former royal estates, but the idea was not followed through. The Long Walk was started during the sovereignty of Charles II (reigned 1660–85), who also replaced the state apartments in the Upper Ward with the present ones, and widened and extended the north terrace.

The next few monarchs had little to do with the castle. After the death of Queen Anne it was actually let out to private individuals, but George III loved it. He commissioned James Wyatt to remodel the exteriors of the upper ward (which were barrack-like and dull) into the Gothic style. He also finally removed Wolsey's tomb from the Lady Chapel, and commissioned the vault where he and most of his family would eventually rest.

But it was George IV (reigned 1820–30) who, aided by Sir Jeffry Wyatt, wrought the greatest changes. He ripped out much of Charles II's works, who, George said, 'brought the vices and fashions of France to disgrace his native soil'. The interiors of the Upper Ward were remodelled and the Round Tower heightened to improve its proportions. Wyatt's architecture has been criticised as 'toy fort' but it has proved practicable over the years, needing little alteration.

Queen Victoria's (reigned 1837–1901) most notable contribution was the Albert Memorial Chapel, and Queen Elizabeth II (reigned 1953–) was forced to restore much of the state apartments, at a cost of £36.5 million, after the disastrous fire of November 1992.

DONNINGTON CASTLE

Donnington is Berkshire's most complete surviving castle, apart from Windsor (and Highclere, which calls itself a castle, but does not look like one as we would understand it). After the story of Windsor, the answer to the question 'who built it?' is delightfully simple.

In 1386 Sir Richard Adderbury was given a 'licence to crenellate and fortify a castle' by Richard II, and erected it just north of Newbury on a hill overlooking a stream of the Lambourn. Sir Richard had been a companion of Edward the Black Prince (the father of King Richard II) at the battles of Crecy and Poitiers.

The ageing, childless Sir Richard sold it in 1415 to Thomas Chaucer, son of the poet and one-time Speaker of the House of Commons in his own right. He used it as a dowry for the marriage of his daughter, Alice. Alice was particularly unlucky in her choice of husbands. The first, Sir John Phellip, died within a year of the wedding; the second, Thomas Montague, Earl of Salisbury, got on the wrong end of a cannon ball at the Siege of Orléans and the third, William de la Pole, Earl of Suffolk, suffered disgrace, banishment and eventually murder by his political enemies, but not before he had fathered a son and several daughters by Alice.

The son, a resolute Yorkist, went on to marry Elizabeth Plantagenet, the sister of Edward IV. Her children were later to be identified as the Yorkist choice as heirs to the throne – a bad career move when the Lancastrian Tudors came to power after the Battle of Bosworth. The heir presumptive met his end at the Battle of Stoke, his brother spent nineteen years in the Tower before being beheaded and the last surviving male of the family died in exile. The Suffolk title and all their property, including Donnington Castle, were naturally confiscated by the King.

Several changes of ownership later (during which time Henry VIII and Elizabeth I are both said to have stayed there), the castle came into the hands of a Mr John Packer, a Puritan Member of Parliament, in 1640. Despite his Parliamentary sympathies, the Royalists seized and occupied it, leading to Mr Packer's comrades in arms twice besieging it, and knocking seven bells out of it in the process. The castle featured large in the Second Battle of Newbury, described in chapter 8. Throughout repeated Parliamentary attacks, the Royalists held onto the castle (or what remained of it) until the end of the Civil War. Little work was, by then, involved for the Parliamentarians to reduce the castle (apart from the gatehouse) to the unfortified, defenceless ruin that exists today. As for Mr Packer, he was given his ruins back, but spent the rest of his days in a town house in Westminster. The remains have been in the care of the state since 1946.

WALLINGFORD CASTLE

Wallingford was Berkshire's most important Anglo-Saxon town (four times the size of Reading), whose leading citizen, Wigod, actually welcomed the conqueror's invasion in 1066. The castle was completed by Wigod's son-in-law, Robert d'Oyly, by about 1071 and, like Windsor, formed part of the conqueror's strategic

defences for London. It dominates a fording point of the Thames, and apparently required the demolition of a good number of high status Anglo-Saxon houses to build it. By the 1130s wood had been replaced by stone, to create 'one of the most powerful royal castles of the twelfth and thirteenth centuries'. Its importance during the twelfth-century civil war between Stephen and Matilda is recorded in chapter 8.

In the thirteenth to fifteenth centuries, the castle (further improved) served both as a royal residence, including for successive dukes of Cornwall and, from 1335 as the principal English residence of the Black Prince.

It also served as a county jail. It may have been hard for attacking forces to break into but, as a jail, it was apparently far too easy to break out of, for there were constant complaints about the number of felons escaping from it.

Its use as a royal residence fell into decline after 1518, the last time that Henry VIII stayed there. The castle was stripped of building materials for use at Windsor Castle and, by 1540, was described by John Leland as 'nowe sore yn ruine and for the most part defaced'.

But its defensive importance came back into its own in the Civil War, when it served as a Royalist outpost against an attack on their main headquarters in Oxford. A new Royalist garrison was installed and the fortifications repaired. They resisted a Parliamentary siege for sixteen weeks in 1646, only surrendering then on very generous terms. The Parliamentary side recognised what a powerful fortress this ancient structure still was and, at the end of hostilities, decided to 'slight it' (that is, virtually reduce it to the rubble you see today). A brick building within it continued to serve as a prison until the eighteenth century (though, without castle walls to keep the villains in, escaping from it must have been even easier than before). Today, what is left of it is both a Grade 1 listed building and a Scheduled Ancient Monument.

HIGHCLERE CASTLE

Better known today as an abbey (the fictional 'Downton Abbey', beloved of television viewers), Highclere calls itself a castle, but is in reality a monumental stately home. Often referred to as being in Berkshire (but actually just across the border in Hampshire), it is built on the foundations of the palace of the bishops of Winchester, who owned the estate from the eighth century, and a nearby Iron Age hill fort is evidence of even earlier settlement at Highclere. It has been the home of the Carnarvon family since 1679.

By the early nineteenth century a Georgian mansion stood there within a landscape created by Capability Brown (a creative process which involved demolishing and relocating an inconveniently situated village and its insufficiently picturesque villagers).

But it was the 3rd Earl who wrought the most dramatic change to the estate. He brought in architect Sir Charles Barry in 1839-42, fresh from his work designing the Houses of Parliament, and commissioned a monumental Jacobean-style mansion, faced in Bath stone, with Italian Renaissance interiors and the odd touches of English Gothic. The west wing and the interior were still far from complete when the earl died in 1849 (Barry followed him in 1860).

The Houses of Parliament, designed by architect Sir Charles Barry.

But the 4th Earl carried on with the help of one of Barry's colleagues, Thomas Allom, and the interiors were finally completed in 1878.

In the twentieth century the house became associated with Egypt. The 5th Earl was an enthusiastic amateur archaeologist, sponsoring digs and accompanying Howard Carter during the discovery of Tutankhamun's tomb in 1922. During the First World War, the house was converted into a hospital for wounded soldiers, and the 5th Countess became a skilled nurse, adored by her many patients.

In the Second World War, the pupils and teachers of the Curzon Crescent Nursery School, Willesden, were amazed to find themselves transported to the stately surroundings of Highclere Castle as evacuees; the library became their playroom, though their dining was strictly limited to the servants' quarters. But the house itself was falling to pieces.

By 2009, only the first and ground floors remained usable; at least fifty rooms were uninhabitable and the 8th Earl and his family were living in a 'modest cottage in the grounds'. Renovations costing £1.8 million were needed on the castle alone, and £12 million was needed for the estate as a whole. Happily, the boom in visitor numbers resulting from the television series has enabled the family to make a start on this backlog.

BASILDON PARK

Records of the Basildon estate date back to the early fourteenth century, but the house itself was first conceived in 1771, when the estate was bought by a Yorkshire man, Sir Francis Sykes. He had made his fortune in India and returned to England to further his political ambitions. The estates he had bought in Yorkshire and Dorset were too remote from the capital to entertain those with political influence, and he looked for something closer to London. This part of Berkshire was ideal for his needs; it was, at the time, so filled with people who had grown rich in India that it was known as 'the English Hindoostan'. The 'nabobs', as these former expatriates were known, came with an unsavoury reputation for looting and oppressing the Indian people. Sykes himself was known as 'Squire Matoot', after a tax he had imposed in Bengal.

His purchase of the estate coincided with a series of financial disasters for him. His shares in the East India Company crashed in value, and financial scandals relating to his conduct both in India and in his British parliamentary constituency resulted in financial loss, public disgrace and the eventual loss of his parliamentary seat. A start on the house was delayed until 1776 and it was still not completed when Sir Francis died in 1804. The house passed to Sir Francis' 5-year-old grandson (also Sir Francis) in that same year, but the Sykes family fortune was almost exhausted and Basildon was already mortgaged. The family's finances were not helped by the new Sir Francis' friendship (as an adult) with the spendthrift Prince Regent, and by 1829 the house was up for sale.

No one was prepared to pay Sykes' asking price of £100,000 and so the family were still there in 1834–35, when Benjamin Disraeli became, first, their house guest and, second, Mrs Sykes' lover. She inspired the central character in his novel *Henrietta Temple: A Love Story*. The evidently sporting Mrs Sykes also took as a lover the painter Daniel Maclise. Maclise was a friend of Charles Dickens, and Sir Francis' treatment of him, in the society scandal which resulted from the affair, led Dickens to base the villainous character of Bill Sykes in *Oliver Twist* on Sir Francis.

The house was finally sold to millionaire entrepreneur James Morrison in 1838, and the interiors were then finally finished. By then, the fashion for Palladian architecture had been supplanted by the neo-classical so, to the purist, the mostly Palladian exterior and neo-classical interiors do not strictly match. It remained in the Morrison family (apart from being requisitioned as a service war hospital in the First World War) until 1929, when it was sold to

Charles Dickens

the first Lord Iliffe. He wanted it for the estate, and put the house, minus most of its land, straight back on the market. The next buyer was property developer George Ferdinando, who hatched the idea of selling the house to a rich American for $1,000,000, dismantling it and rebuilding it in the United States. The idea came to nothing, though some of the house's fixtures and fittings found their way into the Waldorf Astoria Hotel's Basildon Room in New York, and a number of American museums.

During the Second World War, the house was used to billet troops and the remaining land as a prisoner-of-war camp and an army training area (including tank training), none of them ideal uses for the conservation of a historic building. Under the tender care of the government, the lead was stolen from the roof, there was a fire and other damage was inflicted. By 1952, it was said of Basildon Park that 'to say it was derelict is hardly good enough, no window was left intact and most were repaired with cardboard or plywood'.

At this point, the second Lord Iliffe saw the property and was persuaded by his wife to buy it. They embarked on a twenty-five-year programme of restoration, replacing many of the missing fittings with ones from the many country houses that were being demolished at this time (in 1955, they were going at a rate of one every five days). The property was handed over to the National Trust in 1978 and is now protected as a Grade 1 listed building.

READING ABBEY

Reading has a recorded history of settlement that goes back to Saxon times. The first resident known to us by name was Reada, and his followers the 'Readingas', from around AD 600. The town, on the borders of Wessex and Mercia, was fought over by those two kingdoms, and the kings of Wessex (including Alfred the Great) also had to contend with the unwelcome invasion of the Danes, who set up camp in the town around AD 871.

Reading Abbey was founded by Henry I in 1121. It was said he did so in his grief, following the death of his son in the 'White Ship' disaster off the Normandy coast in 1120. It took an age to complete, but Thomas à Becket was able to consecrate the main church in 1164, just six years before he met his death at Canterbury at the hands of Henry's knights. Henry endowed the new church

with many valuables, one of the greatest of which was said to be the preserved hand of the apostle St James. More to the point, he gave the town a spectacular church, larger than Westminster Abbey or Winchester Cathedral, and built in the late Norman style like those at Durham or Gloucester.

The abbey grew to be one of the most powerful and wealthy religious institutions in the country and its abbot a man of considerable importance in both national politics and the life of the town. He sat in the House of Lords; kings and queens accepted his hospitality at the abbey, and locally it was the town's largest employer and the generator of the important pilgrimage traffic. Parliament met there when plague drove it out of London. Locally, the abbot exercised a good deal of control over the town (not always appreciated by the locals). He was Lord of the Manor and acted as a mediaeval town planner cum property developer. For example, the abbot promoted the creation of the Market Place and Friar Street, in order to steal trade from the town's traditional place of business and settlement, around St Mary's Butts.

Come the Reformation, and the dissolution of the abbey inevitably followed in 1539. It was by now the sixth richest religious institution in England. The story of Abbot Hugh Faringdon's principled (if not necessarily well-advised) opposition to Henry's supremacy over the established church is told in the section on Berkshire martyrs. One positive outcome for the town was that Henry VIII granted them a charter in 1542, making them a borough with much wider powers of self-government (if not always the financial means to administer it).

But the abbey church itself was doomed. Its real decline began in the reign of Edward VI, from 1547, when the rapacious Duke of Somerset led the way in stripping it of anything of value. By 1549 the church was largely gutted and roofless. Materials from it went to London, to Windsor (for the castle) and to local projects such as the restoration of St Mary's Church. Centuries of neglect and vandalism followed, until today all we are left with of the church are some of the rubble inner walls (all the dressed stone having been taken). A version of the mediaeval abbey gateway survives, though the decrepit original blew down in a storm in 1861 and was 'restored' in a 'Disneyfied' version by Victorian architect, George Gilbert Scott. Part of the *hospitium*, or pilgrims' hostel also survives, similarly 'improved', both in Victorian times and more recently.

DORCHESTER ABBEY

The village of Dorchester lies at the junction of the rivers Thames and Thame. It is an extremely ancient settlement, with a Roman town and an Iron Age hill fort on nearby Wittenham Clumps. In AD 635 the kings of Wessex gave the Christian missionary (and future saint) Birinus some land there to build a cathedral. Birinus himself was buried there in AD 649 until the threat of war with Mercia led to his remains being moved to the relative safety of Winchester. By the 870s, Dorchester was the centre of a diocese that extended from the Thames to the Humber. This cut no ice with the civil authorities, who made Oxford and Wallingford the area's main military and administrative centres.

Work on the present abbey was started in the twelfth century, though some remnants of the Saxon church, and of the one built by the first Norman bishop, Remigius, after 1070, are to be found in it. It served purely as a parish church until 1140, when it was re-founded as an abbey for Augustinian Canons. It started to become an important place of pilgrimage after 1225, when some remains, supposedly those of St Birinus, were installed there. The income from the pilgrimage trade helped pay for much of the subsequent expansion of the church. All of this came to an end in 1536 when, at the instigation of Henry VIII, the abbey was dissolved and St Birinus' shrine was destroyed. The last abbot, John Mershe, was a man of more flexible views than his counterpart in Reading and by subscribing to the king's supremacy over the church, he earned himself a pension of £22 a year, rather than the attentions of the executioner.

The church escaped the subsequent vandalism suffered by many similar buildings, such as those in Reading, because 'a great riche man' of Dorchester, Sir Richard Bewfforeste, paid Henry VIII £140, the value of the lead on the roof, and thus saved it as a parish church. It has undergone several major restorations over the centuries, the latest of which started in 1998 and is still ongoing.

ABINGDON ABBEY

The area at the junction of the rivers Ock and Thames has been inhabited since at least the Bronze Age. In the seventh century a Saxon nobleman named Hean was given permission (by his uncle Cissa, viceroy of the king of the West Saxons) to build a religious house on some land there.

This proved to be a very bad idea, for the land was yet more disputed territory on the border between the kingdoms of Mercia and Wessex. When the two kings were not fighting over it, river borne marauders came to see what there was to steal, or it was sacked by invading Danes.

The abbey, nonetheless, continued as a small monastery until AD 954, when the king put St Aethelwold, a leading figure in tenth-century monastic life, in charge of it. He also gave him generous gifts of land and money for its upkeep. By the time of Domesday Book the abbey was a major landowner, with forty manors to its name, including large chunks of Berkshire. (In fact, much of Berkshire that was not held directly by the king at that time was in the possession of one or other religious institution.)

Among the improvements carried out by the abbey in the eleventh century was changing the path of the Thames by digging what was called the 'Swift Ditch' to bypass the main channel, thereby enabling barges to reach the abbey. The Thames Commissioners restored the navigation to its original path in 1790, by which time the abbey had long gone.

Edward I and Henry III stayed at the abbey during their respective reigns, and it is suggested that it was there, in about 1301, that Edward I first had the idea of uniting the English and Scottish thrones (about 400 years before it came about).

By the sixteenth century the abbey had a substantial land holding within the centre of Abingdon itself, including a church of some 370ft in length and many associated buildings. But in 1539 they shared the fate of every other such institution under Henry VIII. The last abbot, Thomas Pentecost, alias Rowland, acknowledged the supremacy of the king over the Church in return for his pension, and the abbey was dissolved.

Nothing of the abbey church survives. The fifteenth-century gatehouse to the abbey is complete but 'much restored'. There are some ruinous arches in the Abbey Gardens, but these are apparently Victorian follies, built by a local shopkeeper named E.J. Trendell, using bits of the old abbey or stonework removed from local churches during their nineteenth-century 'restorations'. Some of the ancillary buildings of the abbey are still there, however – the Exchequer, the Long Gallery, the bake house and the *hospitium*, or pilgrims' hostel. The latter was sold to the Corporation, shortly after the dissolution, who at one time used it as a prison that was condemned by penal reformer John Howard. One wing of the hospital was used for a free grammar school between 1563 and 1870 and the Long Gallery at one time formed part of a brewery.

ETON COLLEGE

Henry IV founded what was originally called 'The King's College of Our Lady of Eton beside Windsor' in 1440 (making it the nation's second oldest public school, after Winchester). As well as a school, it was to be a religious and charitable institution. A year later he founded King's College Cambridge, which would be supplied with scholars from Eton (so no worries about selection processes there, then). He endowed it with land and with sacred relics, including parts of the crown of thorns and fragments of the true cross. (There were said to be enough of the latter in circulation across Europe to build an entire galleon.) The Pope was even persuaded to grant the institution the right to grant 'indulgences' (a form of 'get out of gaol free' card for wealthy sinners).

Some important parts of the school were completed by the end of the 1440s, but the church was delayed, first by Henry's interference (he made them knock down the partially completed church in 1448 and replace it with something much grander). A more fundamental problem arose when Henry was deposed in 1461 by the Yorkist Edward IV, who annulled all grants of land and other assets by his Lancastrian rival, which left Eton unfunded. He was persuaded (by his mistress) to restore some of them, but the college had to proceed on a much reduced basis.

The church was completed by 1482, a fine building but only a part of what Henry had originally envisaged. Further additions to the school were made in the sixteenth and seventeenth centuries, and the last major addition was the college library of 1725–29. One oddity from the mid-seventeenth century was that all the boys were required to smoke tobacco each day. This was believed to inhibit the spread of the plague, which was then rampant.

Today the school has grown from the seventy scholars for whom Henry provided, to about 1,300 boys aged between 13 and 18. They are chosen today by competitive examination (and, in 80 per cent of cases, by their ability to afford the fees – in academic year 2010/11 the full fees for the year were £29,862, though bursaries and scholarships were available). There is no longer the option of booking your child's place at birth. One of the school's traditions is its uniform, of black tailcoat and waistcoat, false collar, pinstriped trousers and a white tie. Senior boys can have the privilege of wearing a white bow tie and winged collar. Top hats and walking canes are no longer required, and the beating of boys was phased out in the

1980s. Until 1964, errant boys could receive a 'character forming' semi-public birching of the bare bottom, administered in the library.

The school has produced a host of leading lights in every field of endeavour, including nineteen British prime ministers. Equally interesting is the list of fictional characters who claim to be old Etonians. They include P.G. Wodehouse's Bertie Wooster, the detective Lord Peter Wimsey, Captain Hook from Peter Pan and 007 James Bond (who was allegedly expelled for some unspecified 'trouble' with a young lady).

7

GHOSTS AND GHOULS

A county as ancient as Berkshire has no shortage of ghost stories, and a selection of them are retold here. The author offers no guarantee as to their reliability!

THE DAME OF BISHAM ABBEY

Today Bisham Abbey is the home of the National Sports Centre, but it is also said to be occupied by the ghost of a very eminent lady. The manor of Bisham goes back to the time of Domesday Book and was occupied for a while by the Knights Templar. As an aside, the abbey probably had the shortest life of any similar religious institution. Previously an Augustinian priory, it was declared an abbey in 1537, only to be dissolved by Henry VIII just six months later. The last abbot is said to have placed a curse on the abbey, saying that anyone who subsequently occupied it would suffer premature deaths, particularly of their male line, and there certainly seems to have been a good deal of premature death among those who lived there in later years.

One such was Margaret Pole, the Countess of Salisbury. She was first imprisoned by Henry VIII, ostensibly because her son, Reginald (who just happened to be the Archbishop of Canterbury), chose to criticise the king's policy on religion (never a good career move with Henry VIII). He had the good sense to flee abroad, so the king arrested Margaret and the rest of his family instead. Another reason for their arrest might have been that they were of the Plantagenet bloodline, and therefore might have been rivals for what was not a particularly secure throne. After a period in the Tower, Margaret was executed, but she is not our ghost.

The property was briefly owned by Henry's unloved wife, Anne of Cleves, and eventually passed to a rising star in the diplomatic service, Sir Philip Hoby. He was married to Dame Elizabeth who, in addition to being an academic, and a personal friend and confidante of Queen Elizabeth I, apparently had something of a fixation about death. She buried two husbands and four of her children, and spent an inordinate amount of time in her later years fussing about the arrangements for her own funeral.

She eventually died in June 1609 at the age of 81, and it is her ghost that is said to walk the corridors of Bisham Abbey. As she does so, she constantly washes her hands, apparently in atonement for the murder of one of her sons. It seems he spattered ink all over his writing book and Elizabeth, in a rage, battered him senseless. As further punishment she locked him in a tiny closet. She was then called upon to attend on the Queen and, by the time she returned, he was dead. A sealed-up closet and blotted copybook were found by builders doing renovations in the 1800s.

The abbey stayed in the Hoby family's ownership until 1780, when it was sold to George Vansittart, a man who had made his fortune in India. It was the Vansittart family who bore the brunt, both of the hauntings and of the abbot's earlier curse, as many of the sons of the family met untimely ends. One Vansittart, an admiral, was alone in the abbey one night when he sensed someone behind him. He turned, and found himself face to face with Elizabeth Hoby, dressed exactly as she was in the full-length portrait on the wall – except the frame was now empty, as if she had stepped down from it.

On two separate occasions, dogs who had been sharing the bedroom with their owners have been terrified by an apparition. One of the dogs leapt into bed with its master.

The ghost also appears to have a violent side. Furnishings and clothing have been hurled around the room and the curtains around the bed torn down. On another occasion, a rowing blue stayed there whilst competing at Henley. It seems that he was particularly proud of his fine head of hair, and the wraith threatened to render him bald with a single touch of her finger; the man was so affected by this that he gave up rowing and took up a career in the Church. Dame Elizabeth made a further appearance while the abbey was being used as a wartime military hospital, but has not yet seen fit to trouble the sportsmen and women who now frequent the abbey.

TWO VICTIMS FROM NEWBURY

In 1538 one Thomas Barrie was charged with seditious libel against King Henry VIII. He was arrested at the almshouses at Donnington where he lived, and force-marched to the Market Place in Newbury, where he was placed in the stocks. Barrie was in poor health and the forced march left him very ill, but the captain of the arresting party was a sadist. For him, the humiliation of the stocks was not enough. He had his men attach Barrie to the stocks with two large nails through his ears. Barrie was in agony every time he moved his head, but was left in this state until sunset. He begged the captain to free his ears, but the captain's response was to cut the unfortunate man's ears off. It was the shock of this that finally killed Barrie, and his ghost is now said to wander the Market Place at night.

Near to the Market Place used to stand Pelican Lane, which from 1802 was home to the now disappeared Pelican Theatre. One of its leading actresses was said to have spurned the overtures of a fellow actor. Maddened by the rejection, the actor is said to have stabbed her to death with the suitably melodramatic words 'If I can't have her, no man shall!' Years later the building went into residential use. Those living there used to find that candles mysteriously used to go out at a certain place in the building, only to relight again shortly afterwards. Electric light bulbs also tended to blow when used in that location. One night, they saw a damp patch forming on the ceiling, even though there had been no rain. Liquid began dripping from the ceiling and, when they examined it more closely, it turned out to be blood. The frightened occupiers struggled in vain to clear it up, but were finally forced to admit defeat and went to bed. When they got up in the morning all the traces of blood had gone. It turned out that the room above had been the one where the actress's murder had taken place.

THE LADY OF BUCKLEBURY MANOR AND OTHER LOCAL PHANTOMS

Frances Winchcombe married Henry St John (later Viscount) Bolingbroke in 1701 and, two years later, inherited Bucklebury Manor from her father. Bolingbroke was a leading Tory Member of Parliament, and was responsible for a number of pieces of legislation that made him thoroughly unpopular with everyone but high Tories. He also upset the locals by ordering the cutting down of all the trees around the manor, and was even unpopular with some of the Tories, having fallen out with Prime Minister Robert Harley.

While Queen Anne was on the throne his position was reasonably assured, but when she was succeeded by George I (who deeply mistrusted Tories) in 1715, his position became highly tenuous. He was dismissed from his post and faced trial by the House of Lords for his involvement in a Jacobite plot. Rather than face trial he fled the country, deserting Frances, and became an advisor to the

Queen Anne

exiled Stuart 'pretenders'. She was still besotted with him, and never recovered from his disappearance. She died three years later and is buried in Bucklebury Church. Now it is said that she can be seen riding through the village, weeping bitterly, in a coach drawn by black horses and accompanied by a headless postillion.

Bucklebury appears to be particularly well-endowed with ghosts. Mediaeval monks can apparently be seen at fishponds on the common, and an evil spirit has been known to chase nocturnal visitors down the Devil's Steps. But some of the ghostly manifestations had a more human origin. Sheep stealing and grave robbing were apparently frequent activities in the area, and the robbers would use ghostly imagery to scare away would-be witnesses. One farmer's son was not daunted by this, but lay in wait at night, and was rewarded by seeing a group of eerie-looking coffin bearers leaving the churchyard. He set about them with a club and, having seen them off, found the coffin to contain the dead body – of a stolen sheep.

UNSEEN GHOSTS OF OLD WINDSOR

Some ghosts are heard but not seen. At a
lodge on Priest Hill, Old Windsor, heavy
footsteps are apparently heard, going
upstairs and opening doors. It is thought
to be a former resident, who committed
suicide by tying a lawnmower around
his neck and throwing himself into the
nearby River Thames. There is also a
girl, who makes her presence known
by means of a very sweet scent and
by sitting (unseen) on one's bed.
Her repertoire also includes pulling
off the sleeper's bedclothes and, on
one occasion, burning footprints
into the bedside linoleum. A
Ouija board has been used to
'establish' that her name is
Sally.

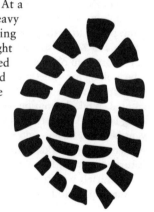

HAUNTINGS IN THE BRACKNELL AREA

Bracknell has no shortage of ghosts:

Kells House was said to be haunted by a monk. People in the house said they could feel him brushing by them and hear the rustle of his robes. The house used to stand in Church Road, but the site of it is now part of a dual carriageway.

A shop in the town apparently used to have its own phantom customer. Shop workers reported seeing a little man, burdened down with parcels and wearing an old-fashioned farmer's smock coat, walking towards the back entrance to the shop. One of them even held the door open for him but instead he walked through the wall. The staff were naturally unnerved by this and even reported the matter to the police, but all they could find out was that the route he was following was along the line of an ancient highway, long since lost to development. The little man took to appearing in the shop on a regular basis, and shop items took to disappearing and reappearing. Eventually, the management called upon the services of a priest, and the little man was seen no more.

The sound of ghostly horses has also been reported on a number of occasions. Demolition workers in the Royal Ascot Hotel heard them, as did people in the Kennel Lane area and Ralph's Ride. The latter was said by one person to be the ghost of Dick Turpin and his horse, Black Bess.

People in Kennel Lane have also reported seeing the ghost of a lady wearing an old-fashioned dove-grey riding habit. She appeared to be looking for something (her horse, perhaps?).

There was also a house in Ralph's Ride that was said to be haunted. While demolition workers were in the house, someone took a dog into it. The beast was terrified – its hair stood on end, its tail went between its legs and it fled from the house. That same night, the demolition workers who were staying in there overnight were disturbed to see a heavy mangle moving across the floor by itself. It was hurled with great force against the opposite wall, and the workers rapidly followed the dog out of the door.

CIVIL WAR GHOSTS FROM THE BATTLE OF NEWBURY

It seems that both sides have left behind witnesses to the First Battle of Newbury. The Earl of Essex, the general leading the Parliamentary forces that day, had his headquarters in Biggs Cottage, Enborne, and it is said that his ghost is to be seen walking the rooms in the cottage. There are also claims of a ghostly sentry being posted outside. For the Royalist side, Lord Falkland, the king's Secretary of State, was fatally wounded in the battle and was brought back to the old manor house at Wash Common to die. His spirit lived on in the house and, apart from human witnesses, dogs were said to refuse to sleep in the kitchen where he died. The site of the old manor house is now a road called Falkland Garth. There are also said to be a group of phantom Royalist cavalry, who ride out to lift the siege at Donnington Castle, only to be attacked by equally spectral Parliamentary forces at nearby Love Lane. For good measure, some of the Earl of Essex's Parliamentary soldiers claimed to have seen a phantom witch crossing the River Kennet near Newbury by a narrow bridge. When they fired on her, the bullets just rebounded off her and nearly hit the shooter.

PHANTOM HIGHWAYMEN

Maidenhead Thicket can lay claim to not one, but two, ghostly highwaymen. In its day it was a notorious area for hold-ups, so much so that clergymen from Henley would demand danger money for conducting services in Maidenhead. One of the highwaymen enjoyed a good deal of popular approval, despite his occupation. Claude Duval was born in Normandy in 1643 and fled to England in 1660 with a price already on his head. In a ten-year career as a highwayman he earned a reputation for being non-violent (insofar as robbery at gunpoint can be non-violent), gallant and a positive

charmer with the ladies. On one famous occasion he is said to have detained a rich man in a coach carrying £400. Duval got the lady accompanying the man in the coach to step out and take a dance with him, whereupon he allowed his victim to keep £300 of his money.

One of Duval's favourite haunts was the Black Boy Inn, near the site of the current library in the centre of Slough (the inn was demolished in 1910). This establishment was so named for a macabre reason, for the landlord had on display the preserved body of a black boy, who had died of consumption and then been dried in an oven to preserve him. Samuel Pepys recalls seeing this grisly exhibit in 1665.

Ten years as a highwayman brought Duval considerable wealth and fame. He had a house in London, a cottage at Lightwater, one at Chobham, a house in Wokingham and one at Sonning. The downside was that it also brought him to prison and the gallows. High society visited him in gaol, but that did not stop the authorities hanging him at Tyburn in January 1670, aged just 27. His earthly remains are buried in Covent Garden Church, with a memorial inscribed 'Here lies Duval. Reader, if male thou art, look to thy purse. If female, to thy heart.' As for his spirit, it is said to frequent the Thicket, no doubt waiting in vain for the next stagecoach.

The area's other phantom highwayman was Captain Hawkes, known as 'the Flying Highwayman' and famed as a master of disguise. But it was disguise that was to be his downfall. Pausing for refreshment at the Rising Sun Inn at Woolhampton, he witnessed a fight developing between two yokels in the bar. When he tried to separate them, they ripped off their smocks to reveal that they were really those predecessors of policemen, Bow Street Runners, who promptly arrested him, leading to his trial and execution.

HERNE THE HUNTER OF WINDSOR FOREST

This is one of the oldest of ghost stories, with variants that go back 1,000 years or more; but this version ties it to the reign of Richard II (1377–99). Herne was a skilled huntsman, in service to Richard, and whose woodcraft was the envy of his fellow huntsmen. Herne and the king were in a hunting party one day when a large stag turned on them. It would have gored the king to death, but Herne intervened and killed the stag, albeit at the cost of a near fatal wound to himself. The other hunters were secretly pleased at the likely demise of the king's favourite. Suddenly, a mysterious stranger appeared on the

scene, saying he was Philip Urswick, a physician who could save
Herne. The king told him to do so, and he cut off the dead stag's
antlers and fixed them to Herne's head. He then had Herne carried to
his hut in the woods.

As soon as they got a chance, the other huntsmen tried to
threaten Urswick, telling him not to save Herne. Urswick said he
could not do this, having promised the king, but he did a deal with
them, that Herne would be saved, but would lose all his skill as a
hunter, provided the other hunters performed a task for Urswick.
All of this duly happened, and an ungrateful king dismissed his now
useless hunter. A distraught Herne rode out into the woods and
hanged himself from an oak tree. The person who found his body
went off to get help but, when he returned, the body was gone. As

they looked for it, the oak tree was struck by lightning and split in two. The story concludes with Herne exacting his ghostly revenge on the other hunters by persuading the king to hang them on Herne's oak. Thereafter, a phantom huntsman wearing a stag's antlers gallops through the woods on a black stallion for all eternity, followed by a pack of baying hounds – the ghostly relics of his fellow hunters.

It is said that the original Herne's oak was accidentally destroyed in 1796, but a replacement, planted in situ by Edward VII in 1906, still stands in a private part of Windsor's Home Park. A version of this story appears in Shakespeare's *Merry Wives of Windsor* (1597), and earlier versions date back to Norse mythology (in which Woden leads the hunt on an eight-legged horse, and regenerates himself by hanging himself on an oak tree). Henry VIII is said to have seen Herne's ghost on two separate occasions, and a more recent sighting of him was reported by a guardsman in 1927, who shortly afterwards shot himself in the Long Walk.

WILD WILL OF LITTLECOTE

Old Mother Barnes was midwife to the village of Great Shefford on the Lambourn Downs. One night in 1557, there was a knock on her door and two mysterious figures summoned her to assist at the birth of a child to a noblewoman. She was taken blindfolded to a great house, which she guessed to be Littlecote Manor, near Hungerford. There she found the woman in labour, and with her was William Darrell, the master of Littlecote. Darrell promised her great rewards if the child was delivered safely, but death if the woman miscarried.

No doubt to her relief, Mother Barnes delivered a healthy boy, which she immediately took to Darrell. To her horror, Darrell snatched the child from her and hurled it into the blazing fire. That night Barnes, who evidently doubled as some kind of a witch, placed a curse upon the Darrell family, that none of its members would live to inherit the Littlecote estate. More practically, she also instituted legal proceedings against Darrell. Though the case against him looked bad, Darrell was able to swing the trial by bribing the judge. He told him that, if he was acquitted, the judge would inherit the estate on Darrell's death.

Sure enough, he got off, but he did not live long to enjoy his freedom. Whilst out hunting one day, he came to leap a fence when the spectre of a baby, engulfed in flames, suddenly appeared before him. It made his horse rear and Darrell was thrown to the ground.

His neck was broken and he died in considerable agony. The estate duly passed to the judge, who lived there for many years.

William's ghost was said to haunt the estate, especially at a place called 'Darrell's Stile'. On dark nights, he was seen riding a huge black horse, with flared nostrils, breath like steam and eyes burning like coals. His travels through the estate were later interrupted when Darrell's Stile disappeared under an American Air Force base in the Second World War.

A NICER CLASS OF GHOST

If any Berkshire building was going to be haunted, it would surely be Windsor Castle, and its spectres would undoubtedly be of a superior nature. Sure enough, the ghosts of former monarchs would seem to be tripping over each other, assuming they had any substance to trip over.

The library seems to be particularly popular. Several of Queen Victoria's children (including the future Edward VII) and the Empress Frederica Germaine are among those who, it is claimed, have seen Queen Elizabeth I there. It has been suggested that her appearances are a portent of war, and that George VI had several encounters with her in the early days of the Second World War.

Keeping her company is George III, who can be heard uttering the words 'What? What?' – allegedly the only ones he said during his periods of madness. Soldiers on guard duty have reported seeing George at the window.

Leaning against a library chair and stroking his beard reflectively is Charles I, whose dead body was brought to the castle after his execution.

Only Henry VIII has forsaken the library for the battlements, where he disappears through a wall, at a place where (ancient plans show) there used to be a door. He has also been reported in the cloisters of the castle, groaning and dragging along the ulcerated leg that would lead to his death in 1547.

Whilst on the subject of the cloisters, a ghostly figure on horseback is said to frequent them, disappearing through a wall. This may be explained by the fact that what are now the cloisters was once the site of the cavalry stables. Henry's second wife, Anne Boleyn (who is buried in London), is said to have appeared at one of the windows of the castle, weeping (so was obviously reunited after death with her severed head).

Queen Victoria

During her lifetime, Queen Victoria and Prince Albert planted a group of spruce trees near the castle. When Edward VIII (encouraged by Wallis Simpson) had them cut down in 1936, it is said that workmen saw the ghostly figure of the old queen intervening to try and save them.

George Villiers, the much hated 1st Duke of Buckingham, is a more surprising visitor to the castle – surprising in that he was murdered, not at Windsor, but in a Portsmouth inn in 1628. Another commoner with more right to be there is William Wykeham, the Surveyor of Royal Castles to Edward III, who masterminded many of the fourteenth-century improvements to the castle. He can be seen in the Round Tower, looking at his handiwork with evident satisfaction. The prison room of the Norman Tower is said to be occupied by an unidentified Royalist prisoner, no doubt rather less satisfied with his surroundings.

WINDSOR'S COMMONER GHOSTS

If the castle is the preserve mainly of aristocratic ghosts, the commoner variety have to reside in the town itself. Several properties in Thames Street are said to be particularly haunted, with shop assistants working in one being tapped on the shoulder or nudged, and others, in Curfew House, feeling a strong urge to throw themselves down the stairwell.

People sleeping in yet another property reported nightmares of a horrible old man, another one dragging his lame leg behind him, trying to strangle them. To add to its gruesome reputation, a thick, black musty smelling vapour used to permeate parts of the house, and the charred remains of several babies were said to have been found under the floor. It is rumoured to be the house where Cardinal Wolsey stayed, after his fatal falling out with Henry VIII, and his ghost was seen, walking through it (literally) on two occasions in the 1920s.

One of the rooms in the Old House Hotel on Thames Street near the bridge is also said to be haunted, so much so that the London staff of one owner, Baroness Vaux, refused to work there and she had to hire in local servants.

Hadleigh House in Sheet Street was similarly affected. Residents reported 'unwelcome feelings' and inexplicable footsteps on the stairs and, on one occasion a door was locked from the inside of an empty room with no other means of access. At another time, the dining room was filled with the sound of knocking all around the room and the overwhelming scent of clove carnations. Years later, a different occupier, who knew nothing of this story, had a very similar experience.

Elsewhere in Sheet Street, in Old Institute House, a Mr Bentley, a former CID officer (and not easily impressionable), used to be conscious of a marked drop in temperatures on a landing in his flat. One night, as he was preparing to go to sleep, he found himself confronted by a figure, lit by moonlight and with huge staring eyes, who vanished when he turned the bedside light on. Mr Bentley has also confronted figures dressed as Cromwellian puritans in the garden of his house, formerly part of the grounds of an ancient property, Abbey House.

Turning to public buildings, Windsor's Theatre Royal is an Edwardian structure, replacing one which burned down in a fire in 1908. It is said to be haunted by the ghost of a girl called Charlotte, who died in the fire, while the former operating theatre at the King Edward VII Hospital is said to be where the late surgeon, Sir Joseph Skeffington, appears. The former Playhouse Cinema (now demolished) experienced numerous paranormal events, including a ghostly woman in a long dress, who used to appear on the stage. One theory is that this has to do with an unsolved murder that took place in a bicycle shop that had previously stood on the site.

A GHOSTLY PHOTOGRAPH

H.E. Luxmore was a long-standing master at Eton College. After his death, friends erected a pavilion in his honour and commissioned a photograph to commemorate its opening. When it was developed, the unmistakeable figure of the late Mr Luxmore, with his stick, cape and flowing white hair, could be seen standing among the guests.

Elsewhere in Eton, the fifteenth-century Old Cock Pit Inn boasts a ghostly lady in grey, who passes quietly between the tables. In a nearby flat, the woman seen walking 18in above the floor puzzled observers until it was realised that the floor in the room concerned used to be much higher.

HAUNTED HOSTELRIES

The Ostrich Inn, Colnbrook

If a ghost is looking for somewhere to spend eternity, a public house might be as good a choice as any. The Ostrich Inn at Colnbrook is the third or fourth oldest licensed house in the country, depending on who you ask – yet others think it far less ancient (the name is apparently a corruption of 'hospice', rather than a reference to the bird). Highwaymen Claude Duval and, inevitably, Dick Turpin are said to have frequented it, Turpin allegedly leaping from a window to evade the clutches of the Bow Street Runners. Its antiquity and chequered history (see the section on murders) make it a likely candidate for hauntings.

Mark Bourne, who managed the pub in modern times, was a sceptic before taking the job, but said that 'strange noises, ghostly figures and objects moving by themselves are all in a day's work' there. A woman in Victorian dress and a young girl are two of the spectral figures that frequent the place. Equipment is mysteriously switched on and off, and cold spots and feelings of despair are reported, particularly in the room where the murder victims were said to have been stored. Mr Cole, the final murder victim, is also said to have made it his post-death local.

Small wonder that the pub has been studied by the Sussex Paranormal Research Group. In 2003, it hosted an overnight stay by seventeen members of the Ghost Club who, unsurprisingly, found themselves surrounded by spirits (and not just the ones that come in bottles). One of the group got to know 'John', who had lived around the time of Queen Elizabeth I, and it was discovered that a particular chair could affect the personality, or even the appearance, of anyone who sat in it.

Nearby the Ostrich Inn was the Toll House (until 1962, when it was demolished), where Dick Turpin was said to have shot a former keeper, John Pearce. Pearce's spirit was said to walk the site at Halloween.

THE ROYAL STAG AND THE UNSEEN HAND

One winter's day in the late nineteenth century, a labourer was returning from a job in Taplow with his son. He decided to stop in the Royal Stag, in Datchet, to slake his thirst. He was not allowed to bring his son into the bar, despite it being a bitterly cold day, and left him outside. As he grew ever colder, the child tried desperately to catch his father's attention by pressing his hand against the pub window, but his father was too engrossed in his ale to pay him any attention. By the time he remembered his son, the boy was dead from exposure.

Thereafter, a spectral handprint used to appear from time to time on the pub window. In 1979, a national newspaper published a photograph of the handprint and brought in scientists to explain the phenomenon; they were gratifyingly baffled. A photograph of the handprint was left on the bar overnight and, when he came down in the morning, the landlord found it covered with broken glasses and bottles. Naturally, none of this smashing had been heard by the landlord or his family overnight.

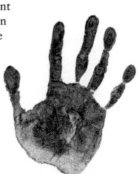

SOME OTHER GHOSTLY LOCALS

The Hobgoblin pub in Maidenhead's High Street is said to be frequented by a poltergeist called Bob, who moves coats, makes money disappear and reappear and turns beer taps on and off.

The Moat House Hotel at Sindlesham has had a chequered history. It was a nineteenth-century mill house, but has also been at various times a workhouse, a church and the home of the Poachers public house, at which the ubiquitous Dick Turpin apparently once drank. All sorts of paranormal activities have been reported – lights switching on and off, the sounds of children laughing, and a coach and horses arriving – some of which has been captured on tape.

The George Inn – a former coaching inn at the junction of King Street and Minster Street, Reading, dating from 1423 or earlier, is said to be occupied by the ghost of a Civil War cavalier.

MODERN GHOSTS

A ghostly blue car has been seen on Berkeley Avenue, Reading. It has no lights and makes no sound, but the driver is clearly visible – a good-looking red-haired woman with her hair piled high.

In Langley, the local almshouses were once used to house Second World War evacuees. A local lady, a Mrs Briggs, objected to what she saw as the misuse of these properties, and said that, if she died, she would come back and haunt them until they were restored to their proper use. Sure enough she passed away and the tenants started reporting poltergeist activity – furniture being moved and bedclothes pulled off sleepers. It was only stopped after the house was subject to an exorcism.

8

BATTLEFIELD BERKSHIRE

In this chapter we will look at some of the battles that have been conducted in the fields (and, in one case, streets) of Berkshire over the centuries. Plus one that rather stretches the definition of 'Berkshire', by some thousands of miles.

THE BATTLE OF ASHDOWN: 8 JANUARY AD 871

Some of the details of this battle are unclear – for example, exactly where it took place. Accounts of it are largely based on Asser's *Life of King Alfred*, written in about AD 893 by a Welsh monk who became Alfred's biographer and Bishop of Sherborne. The term 'Ashdown' relates to all the Berkshire Downs, but among the favourite locations for the battle are Thorn Down, at Compton near East Ilsley (the name means 'place of conflict'), or somewhere on the Ridgeway between Aldworth and the Astons.

Danish forces invaded in AD 870 and, having established a base where the rivers Thames and Kennet join at Reading, set about attacking the West Saxon communities. Raiding parties were sent out towards Aldermaston. They met with Aethelwulf, the Ealdorman of Berkshire (the king's deputy), at Englefield and, with the support of King Ethelred and his brother Prince Alfred, the Danes were beaten and driven back to Reading.

Seeking to capitalise on their victory, the Saxons attacked the Danish fortifications at Reading, but were driven back. They retreated onto the Berkshire Downs with the bulk of the Danish Army in hot pursuit. At the top of Blowingstone Hill (Kingstone Lisle) lay a large perforated sarsen stone. If blown into correctly, this could apparently produce a loud booming noise, and legend has it that

Alfred used this signal to summon his fellow Saxons from all over the Downs. He rallied them at a hill fort near Ashdown House, while Ethelred's men assembled at nearby Hardwell Camp and the Danes made camp at Uffington Castle.

On 8 January about 800–1,000 West Saxons squared up to a slightly smaller Danish force, somewhere on the Downs. Ethelred chose this moment to disappear off to a church service, to pray for victory, leaving the armies in the charge of his 21-year-old brother, Alfred. Alfred could see that the Danes were manoeuvring into an advantageous position, and decided to launch his attack without waiting for his brother to return. As his biographer put it: '... acting courageously, like a wild boar ... and strengthened by divine help, when he had closed up the shield wall in proper order, he moved his army without delay against the enemy'.

Battle was joined and apparently there were heavy casualties on both sides. The Danes lost their King Bagsecg, and five earls. They retreated back to Reading and the West Saxons celebrated a great victory. Their triumph was short-lived, however. Soon afterwards, the Danes won victories at Basing and at Merton, where Ethelred was fatally wounded and Alfred succeeded him as king.

Peace would finally be made with the Danes in AD 878, and in the 880s a series of fortified sites, or burhs, were built throughout Wessex, to help repel any future invaders. This did not prevent a further influx of Vikings in 1006, during which they feasted at Christmas, in Reading on plundered food and drink, and burnt Wallingford to the ground.

THE ANARCHY: 1139–1153

England had another civil war, long before the unpleasantness involving Oliver Cromwell and Charles I, and Berkshire was heavily involved in the action. Shortly before his death in 1135, Henry I asked his barons to support his daughter, Matilda, as the rightful heir to the throne. They agreed at the time, but later reneged on the agreement, backing Stephen, a grandson of William the Conqueror, who usurped the throne on Henry's death. This led to Matilda invading England in 1139 (she was married to Geoffrey of Anjou and lived in France) and the start of a period of civil war known as 'the Anarchy'.

At this time, Wallingford Castle was a very powerful fortification in a key location. In 1139 its owner, Brien Fitzcount, changed sides and became a supporter of Matilda. Wallingford Castle became the easternmost point of the area she controlled. Its importance grew in 1141, after Oxford fell to Stephen and Matilda took shelter at Wallingford. Stephen initially tried to besiege Wallingford Castle, but soon realised that its defences were impregnable, and instead built castles of his own – at Crowmarsh Gifford, Brightwell, South Moreton and Cholsey – in an attempt to contain its activities.

King Stephen

Further attempts to take the castle were made by Stephen in 1145/46 and 1152.

The castle contained a notorious prison, called Brien's Close, and the screams from its tortured prisoners kept the residents of the adjoining town awake.

By 1153 the garrison at Wallingford was running low on food, and a deal was struck with Stephen to allow Brien and his men to leave. This prompted Matilda's son, Henry (the future Henry II), to march there and put Stephen's castles under siege. The two sides squared up to each other outside Wallingford Castle but, rather than fight, brokered a temporary peace deal called the Treaty of Wallingford that would eventually lead to the end of the civil war.

There was another castle, at Hamstead Marshall, just west of Newbury. It was owned by John Marshal, another supporter of Matilda, and Stephen put him under siege in 1152. This time Stephen was holding what he thought was a trump card, in the form of John's young son, William, as a hostage. He threatened to hang the child in full view of the castle unless John surrendered, but the doting father replied 'I still have the hammer and the anvil with which to forge more and better sons.' Not even Stephen's threat to fire young William, alive, into the castle with his trebuchet (giant siege catapult) melted the cold heart of William's father.

In the event, Stephen did not have the heart to harm young William. This was just as well, as William Marshal grew up to be the greatest soldier and diplomat of his era, and served the nation well, including as regent to the child king, Henry III, from 1207 (see the chapter on notable people associated with Berkshire).

CIVIL WAR

The First Battle of Newbury: 20 September 1643
The Thames Valley was one of the key battlegrounds of the Civil War, with the Parliamentary headquarters in London at one end, and the Royalist stronghold in Oxford at the other. After the failure of the Parliamentarians to gain a decisive victory at Edgehill (1642), the Royalists advanced on London, capturing Banbury, Oxford and Reading along the way.

Once the Earl of Essex had laid siege to the Royalist garrison at Reading, the war reached something of a stalemate, with neither side able to strike a decisive blow – the Royalists were short of supplies and ammunition, while the ranks of the Parliamentarians were decimated by disease. Defeats elsewhere meant that Essex's army was the only Parliamentary force left in the field, and he urgently sought reinforcements from London.

The Royalists, meanwhile, were besieging Gloucester and, once he had been reinforced, Essex set off to relieve the city. His arrival there was enough to lift the siege but, having done this, a shortage of supplies left Essex with no choice but to head back to London. This he did and, after a slow start, the Royalist army under the command of King Charles himself set off after them.

To avoid an encounter with the superior Royalist cavalry in open ground, Essex decided that his route to London would be via Newbury. The Royalists made better progress than their opposition, who wrongly assumed that Charles had given up on the battle and was making for his headquarters in Newbury. This, plus some delaying skirmishes by Prince Rupert's cavalry and an encounter with a swamp, delayed Essex so much that the Royalists were able to reach Newbury first and block the road to London. The Parliamentarians arrived soon after and, both sides being too exhausted to fight, pitched camp for the evening.

Important though the battle was, it is very hard to establish what happened, since there exists no contemporary plan of the battlefield, no written record of either side's tactics and the accounts of the battle written by either side were contradictory. What we do know is that the two sides were roughly equally matched – the Royalists had 7,000 cavalry and 7,500 infantry, and the Parliamentarians 6,000 cavalry and 8,000 infantry. Casualties were also fairly equal – 1,300 Royalists and 1,200 Parliamentarians.

Essex had an early success, capturing the strategically important Round Hill, from where 1,000 musketeers could pour fire down on the advancing Royalists, and the Royalists suffered heavy casualties trying to retake it. The fighting was brutal – one Parliamentary sergeant recalled that, as the cannons fired on them, men's bowels and brains flew in their faces. Royalist cavalry mounted repeated charges on the opposing infantry, but they were resisted resolutely by musket and pike. The king's Secretary of State, Viscount Falkland (who also makes an appearance in the chapter on ghosts), was killed by a musket ball in the stomach as he tried to charge through a gap in a hedge.

Battle raged for twelve hours but, by nightfall, the Royalists were virtually out of gunpowder and had no choice but to quit the field. The road was open for Essex to continue his progress to

Aldermaston and thence to London (where he was greeted as a hero). The Royalists were left to gather up their dead and wounded (the most senior Royalist fatalities were buried in Newbury Guildhall) before returning to Oxford.

This battle is reckoned by some historians to be a decisive moment in the Civil War, where the high point in the Royalists' fortunes was thrown into reverse by their defeat.

The Second Battle of Newbury: 27 October 1644

King Charles had been fighting in the West Country, but returned to relieve the besieged Royalists in Donnington Castle, near Newbury. There he met with Prince Rupert, who gave him an account of their recent defeat at Marston Moor. The Earl of Essex was bearing down on them, in charge of three Parliamentary armies, and Charles ordered Rupert to go into Gloucestershire, in hopes of dividing the Parliamentary forces. In the event, the Parliamentarians did not fall for the ploy, which therefore had the effect of dividing the Royalist, instead of the Parliamentarian armies. Donnington was relieved on 22 October, and Charles waited at Newbury for Rupert to return and for another contingent under the Earl of Northampton to join him.

Charles occupied three strong points – Shaw House, east of Newbury, where some Iron Age embankments formed part of the defences; Donnington Castle to the north and Speen, to the west. The River Kennet was an obstacle to the south and the River Lambourn separated Speen and Newbury from Shaw and Donnington.

On 26 October the Parliamentary forces advanced to Clay Hill and set up their artillery. Essex was ill, so command was split between the generals of the two other armies, Sir William Waller and the Earl of Manchester. They decided to divide their forces, with Manchester attacking Shaw, and Waller performing a flanking movement to attack Speen from the west. Waller's cavalry was led by a farmer from Huntingdon, one Oliver Cromwell.

Speen was defended by troops under Prince Maurice, the brother of Prince Rupert. They were out foraging when the attack came, and were taken totally by surprise. Speen fell to the Parliamentarians, but Shaw House resisted Manchester's attack. However, Charles felt sufficiently defeated to order a retreat back to Oxford, leaving behind his wounded and most of his guns and baggage. The Parliamentarians failed to block his retreat and only pursued him when it was too late to catch him. Instead the generals ordered a hastily improvised attack on Donnington Castle, which the Royalist occupants repelled, with many Parliamentary casualties. Charles returned a week or two later and raised the siege at Donnington for a second time.

The battle produced a tactical win for the Parliamentarians, but failed to give them any strategic advantage. The Parliamentary Council of War was divided and defeatist at this point. The Earl of Manchester said:

> The King need not care how oft he fights ... if we fight a hundred times and beat him 99 he will be king still, but if he beats us but once, or the last time, we shall be hanged, we shall lose our estates and our posterities be undone.

To which Cromwell replied:

> If this be so, why did we take up arms at first? This is against fighting ever hereafter. If so, let us make peace, be it ever so base.

Criticism from Cromwell and others of the half-hearted conduct of the war would lead to Essex, Manchester and Waller all losing their commands and the formation of the New Model Army, modelled on Cromwell's Ironsides and trained in Windsor Great Park. They would win a decisive victory at the Battle of Naseby the following June.

SIEGE

Civil War Reading: 1642–49

Reading was a key centre of communications during the Civil War and, as such, was fought over by both sides. In addition to its strategic position, it was seen as a relatively large and (it was falsely assumed) prosperous community that could help fund each side's war effort.

Reading itself had divided loyalties, and some of its leading families – like the Vachels – even had family members on both sides. From June 1642 the town was occupied by a relatively small Parliamentary garrison, but they quit the town hurriedly on the news that a much larger force, under the personal command of the king, was advancing on the town. Some of the town's Parliamentary families, like that of John Milton's brother, Christopher, also took the opportunity to get out.

Charles' army stayed briefly, exercising a reign of terror in which they extracted what they could from the local townspeople. They then left for London, leaving the town garrisoned by 3,000 infantry, 300 cavalry, a few cannon and very little gunpowder. They were under the command of Sir Arthur Aston, a great and notorious papist, of whom it was said that he had the fortune to be very much esteemed where he was not known, and very much detested where he was.

He set about catholicising the town and turning it into a fortress, erecting large earthworks the size of houses where the rivers did not provide their own protection. The ruins of Reading Abbey and the town's supply of wool bales provided a plentiful supply of building materials for the fortifications, and Aston had no hesitation in vandalising the rest of the town in the name of security. In particular, he turned Caversham Bridge into a rickety improvised drawbridge that could be lifted at night.

The town's economy was crippled, and was not helped by the heavy demands for funding, made by the occupying forces. People in Reading in 1642–43 found themselves paying 15 shillings in taxes for every penny they had previously paid, and the town's remaining clothiers found themselves making soldiers' uniforms, for which they would never get paid. Troops were billeted on the town, leading to overcrowding and the spread of disease. The troops themselves were ill-trained and ill-disciplined, and Aston had to deploy the better trained part of them guarding the rest.

In April 1643, the Earl of Essex, with a Parliamentary army of 16,000 and some huge cannon, arrived to lay siege to the town. If conditions were bad for the Royalist soldiers in their overcrowded billets, they were infinitely worse for the besieging Parliamentary troops, who generally had no shelter and were reduced to sleeping under hedges and in ditches. Typhus was rife among both armies and the civilian population of Reading.

Essex invited Aston to surrender the town or he would beat it about his ears. Aston declined, the siege began and Aston was soon among those put out of action, in his case by a dislodged roof tile landing on his head. The defenders, short of gunpowder and munitions, attempted to bring in fresh supplies, but were thwarted by Parliamentary intelligence about their plans. King Charles himself led a force to relieve the town, which foundered in a firefight in Caversham.

Surrender terms were negotiated, under which Aston's second in command, Richard Feilding, was able to march his troops out of the town. Feilding was actually sentenced to death (later reprieved) for agreeing his surrender terms, which included handing back to the Parliamentarians for summary execution any Parliamentary troops who had deserted to the Royalist cause.

The Parliamentary troops that replaced the Royalists as an occupying force were no more gracious guests than their predecessors, demanding further contributions from the town towards their war chest. A large force was billeted on the town from 1646–49, accompanied (as if further misfortune were needed) by an outbreak of plague. Only by 1652 were most of the fortifications in the Forbury levelled, and life began returning to something approaching normal. The mound in Forbury Gardens is thought to be the last surviving vestige of those fortifications.

As for Sir Arthur Aston, he recovered sufficiently to take command of the garrison at Oxford, where he proved so unpopular that even his own men beat him up one night. He eventually met his end as Governor of Drogheda in Ireland, in 1649, when Parliamentary forces beat out his brains with his own wooden leg and cut him into pieces.

Berkshire had been one of the nation's more prosperous counties, but was largely ruined by the war. Parliament in June 1645 approved a collection in London's churches for the relief of the 'poor distressed people' in Abingdon, and there were tax riots in Reading in 1647. If this were not enough, the troops had also brought with them typhus, dysentery and possibly also the plague when they were billeted on civilian populations. Areas throughout the county suffering these unwelcome visitations from troops saw death rates rise to two, three or even four times their usual level.

FIGHTING IN THE STREETS: READING, 9 DECEMBER 1688

On the death of King Charles II in 1685, his brother James succeeded to the throne. He was widely unpopular, on account of his Catholic leanings. At first it seemed that his opponents could sit tight and wait for a more sympathetic monarch to take his place, but when he produced a male heir, the prospect of a Catholic succession seemed all too real. Whigs and Tories united to invite James' son-in-law, the Dutch William of Orange, to come and remove James from the throne. William landed in Torbay in November 1688 and marched on London.

James had several hundred Irish Catholic troops stationed in Reading. The locals hated and feared them. When William's troops reached Hungerford, the authorities in Reading sent out a message, seeking his help, and William sent 250 Dutch troops to relieve the town. The Irish were expecting them, and they posted lookouts in the tower of St Mary's Church, looking westward in the direction of the Bath Road. Cavalry were placed in Castle Street, and other troops were stationed in St Mary's churchyard, Broad Street and in Market Place. The locals got wind of this, and sent a further message to the advancing Dutch. Instead of advancing up the Bath Road and into a trap, they switched to the Oxford Road, and were able to catch the Irish troops by surprise.

A full scale battle was staged in the streets of Reading. The Dutch drove the Irish back along Minster Street and Broad Street, and corralled them with the main body of their force in Market Place. Here, local people joined in the fray, firing on the Irish from the upper floors of their houses. The Irish failed to realise that they outnumbered their opponents and fled in the general direction of Twyford, with the Dutch in hot pursuit. In total, about fifty-three of the Irish were killed or wounded, for the loss of six Dutchmen. Some of the dead are buried in St Giles' churchyard. For a century afterwards, Reading's church bells were rung on the anniversary of the battle. As for James, he fled to France, bringing to a conclusion the so-called 'Bloodless Revolution' – bloodless, that is, except in Reading.

CIVIL DISORDER: CAPTAIN SWING, 1830–31

Civil disorder can also provoke a military response and turn our green and pleasant land into a battlefield. Agricultural labourers in Berkshire were having a hard time of it in the late eighteenth and early nineteenth centuries. Their pay was some of the lowest in the country – a full week's work would barely sustain an average family for four or five days, forcing them to seek parish relief. There were bread riots in Newbury in 1766, Thatcham in 1800 and Windsor in 1804.

At that time, there was no professional police force to maintain order, and serious disturbances had to be dealt with either by the regular army or the county militias. These latter were established by an Act of 1757 (one of the times when a French invasion was feared). Each county and its parishes were held responsible for recruiting and equipping a set number of troops (Berkshire's quota was 565 ordinary soldiers). Members of the public were chosen by lot to serve a three-year term, involving a few weeks' training a year and a call-out whenever domestic or foreign threats loomed. One of the first call-outs for the Berkshire force was to help quell the Newbury bread riots.

Even less fully trained were the voluntary corps that were authorised under an Act of 1793. Several of these corps were formed in Berkshire. One of them, the Woodley Cavalry, was under the command of Henry Addington, Speaker of the House of Commons and future prime minister, and another, the Thatcham Corps, were also called out to help break up a group of 400 demonstrators who assembled in Thatcham in 1800, demanding higher wages or cheaper food.

The 'Captain Swing' riots of 1830–31 demanded the attention of all of the forces of law and order. At this time, the agricultural labourers' already miserable lot was being made worse by the introduction of labour-saving mechanical threshing machines. The Captain Swing protests extended across much of southern England and beyond. They started out with letters of protest to individual farmers against the new machines, many of them signed by the fictitious Captain Swing and making threats against the farmer's

machinery, or even his person. (For all the blood-curdling content of the protest letters, there is a record of only one person dying during the riots, and that was a protester, at the hands of a militia man.)

There were, in total, some 200 'Swing' incidents in Berkshire, including about eighty cases of threshing machine destruction. The first occurred in November 1830 at Colnbrook and Holyport, when the yeoman cavalry of three counties had to be called out to protect farmers who had been threatened. For good measure, landowning interests in the area formed the Forest Association for the Apprehension of Felons.

Later that month, a mob of several hundred workers assembled in Thatcham and, after their threatening letters had had no effect, went from farm to farm at Bucklebury, Bradfield, Stanford Dingley, Beenham, Aldermaston and Brimpton for a couple of days, smashing up threshing machines and burning hayricks. The estates of prominent politicians, including the Duke of Wellington and Charles Dundas, MP for Berkshire, were singled out. They also attacked iron foundries where the offending machines were made.

At Brimpton, the rioters were met by a force comprising constables, the local MP, gentleman farmers and workers who sided with their employers. Eleven rioters were initially arrested and both the local militia and the Grenadier Guards regulars were called in to help round up the rest of the ringleaders. They cast their net fairly wide, for a total of 162 Berkshire men were eventually brought before special sessions of the County Assizes. Of these, seventy-eight were gaoled or sentenced to transportation, though only one of the twenty-seven sentenced to death (a William Winterbourne) was actually hanged.

... AND AN AWAY MATCH: MAIWAND, 27 JULY 1880

There is a corner of a Reading field that is forever Afghanistan, to misquote the poet. No more striking memorial to Berkshire's involvement in war can surely exist than the gigantic lion that stands guard over Reading's Forbury Gardens. It commemorates a heroic last stand by the 66th (Berkshire) Regiment of Foot and others, in which 286 of the Berkshires were killed and another thirty-two wounded.

It took place during the Second Afghan War of 1878–80. The war resulted from Russia sending an uninvited and unwelcome diplomatic mission to Afghanistan. The Afghans tried but failed to prevent it entering their country. Britain was Russia's great rival in the Middle East and we said that, if Russia were sending an uninvited and unwelcome diplomatic mission, we wanted to send one as well. When the Afghans refused to let it in, Britain sent an uninvited and unwelcome army instead.

The British (and their Indian allies) initially did rather well, winning a number of victories. On 26 July word came through that an Afghan force was making for the Maiwand Pass, and an Anglo-Indian force of about 2,500 men under Brigadier General George Burrows was dispatched to intercept them. What they did not know was that this was the main Afghan force, that it outnumbered them by about ten to one and that it was equipped with some very modern (British made) artillery.

In the engagement, the Indian troops on the left flank fell away, exposing the 66th to the full force of the Afghan attack. A determined last stand was staged, by some of the remnants of the 66th and some Bombay Grenadiers, at a garden in a place called Khig. When only eleven of them were left, they mounted a heroic, but utterly futile, charge (in the finest British tradition) on the massed ranks of the enemy. In total, almost 1,000 of the Anglo-Indian force was lost, compared to 2,000–3,000 Afghans.

Both sides were disappointed at the outcome of the battle – the British because they lost, and the Afghans because they gained so little from their costly victory (which was in any event reversed by the Battle of Kandahar, later that same year). The British were also miffed at having lost their colours at the battle, which led to an end to the practice of taking them on active service.

But the battle (and its heroics) were widely celebrated at home. Kipling and William McGonagall both wrote ballads about it, several paintings of the 66th's last stand were commissioned and there was even a monument raised to Bobbie, the regiment's canine mascot, who was found limping back from the scene of the battle. (Having survived the battle, Bobbie met his end under the wheels of a hansom cab in Gosport in 1882). In the world of fiction Sherlock Holmes' Dr Watson was also described as having been wounded at Maiwand, and it was thought Arthur Conan Doyle may have modelled him on the 66th's medical officer, Surgeon Major Alexander Francis Preston.

The Forbury Lion was paid for by public subscription and designed by George Blackall Simonds, the sculptor member of the local brewing family (who also made the Queen Victoria statue outside Reading Town Hall). It is said to be the world's largest

sculpture of a standing lion (at 31ft long by 13ft 11in high) and is also claimed by some to be standing in an anatomically impossible pose for a lion (despite Simonds having made extensive life drawings of live lions). It weighed some 16 tons and had to be transported to Reading in pieces, because Reading's rickety bridges could not cope with the whole thing in one go. Unfortunately, Reading did not lavish as much attention on its live heroes as it did its dead ones. Thomas Weston, one of only thirteen survivors of Maiwand, had been expected to live on a pension of just 9½*d* a day, until the public raised a subscription to set him up in business as a chimney sweep.

9

WHY IS IT CALLED THAT?

I approach this part of the book with particular trepidation. There is a great deal of scholarship and detective work involved in the unravelling of ancient place names. To name but one source, the English Place-Name Society (EPNS) devotes itself to these studies and, to my knowledge, has published at least three learned volumes just on Berkshire's place names. To my untutored eye, much of these books appear to be written in Old English or code. Or, to put it another way, any reader with a serious interest in place names is strongly recommended to go back to the authoritative sources and study them in depth.

So, with this health warning in mind, here is my attempt to fathom out why some of Berkshire's places are called what they are. Some place names not dealt with here may be found in the sections of the book dealing with that particular part of Berkshire.

Place names tend to break down into categories. Some are what they call 'habitative', in that they have as their main component words for a village, farm or hamlet. Examples may end in 'ton', 'ham', 'cot', 'worth', 'thorpe' or 'stead' (respectively meaning a fenced place, a farm or homestead, a cottage or small building, an enclosure, a secondary settlement, and a place or enclosed pasture). 'Topographical' names tell you something about the environment, rather than the settlement itself: examples may end in 'don', 'more' or 'ford' (a hill or down, a pond, and a ford or crossing). Yet others refer to people or groups of people who occupied particular areas (like the Readingas, followers of Reada, who were the first recorded group to occupy what is now Reading; or Esgar, an official from the time of Edward the Confessor, whose name survives in East Garston (formerly Esgareston).

Here are some common components of place names that may help you decipher ones I have missed:

-arbor	a tree
Bear- (or **Bere-**)	woodland swine pastures
Been-	land on which beans were grown
-burn (or **-bourne**)	a brook
-bury	a fort. Could be an Iron Age hill fort, as at Blewbury, or a moated Anglo-Saxon manor house, as at Kintbury.
-caster, -cester, -ceaster	from *castrum*, a fortress
-clere	hill, as in Highclere or Burghclere
-col	from the Latin for hill
-cot	cottage or small dwelling
-dun (or **-don**)	a low hill or down
-ey	an island of dry ground surrounded by streams
-field (OE **feld**)	denotes open land (implicitly as distinct from mountain, marsh or woodland). Possibly former woodland cleared for cultivation.
-ford	ford or crossing
-ham	the earliest term for a village or enclosure. Others, like **-cot** and **-worth**, came later. (But 'hamm', spelt thus, can mean land in a river bend.)
-holt	a copse
-hurst	a wood
-ing	belonging to
Leck-	land where leeks or garlic grows
-ley (OE **leah**)	denotes a special association with woodland. It has several meanings, most commonly a woodland clearing.
-low (or **-hloew**)	a grave mound
-mere or -more	a pond, for example in the chalk uplands

Pinge-	place at the end of a wood
-stead	place, enclosed pasture
-street, -stone or -stretton	names connected to places near a Roman road (for example, Paley Street near Bray)
Swin-	land on which pigs were kept
-ton (or -tun)	a fenced place
-thorpe	a secondary settlement
-ton	a large farm or estate granted to an important official
Walh-	having to do with the Welsh
-well	a spring
-wick	could come from the Roman '*vicus*', for a small Roman settlement, or from a Saxon word for a dairy farm (as in Braywick or Eton Wick).
-worth	enclosure
Double-barrelled names	in some cases, the Normans added their own family name to the earlier name for a place. For example, Hampstead Norris, or Sutton Courtenay.

BERKSHIRE?

To begin with Berkshire itself. According to some sources, the name first appears in AD 860 and Asser, the tenth-century Bishop of Sherborne, says it comes from a large forest of box trees, named Bearroc (itself from a Celtic word meaning 'hilly'). The location of this forest is unclear, but one suggestion is the clay lands between Enborne and Hungerford. Other suggestions are that the name 'Berroc seyre' derives from the Bibroci, a group who used to live in the western end of the county, or from 'beorce' (or beech), the trees that flourished in its woodlands. The name Berrocscire appears in a charter of King John, dated 1199, and there is a reference in it to a wood of the same name.

Some Rivers

Enborne	alder stream
Kennet	the name is British and stems from 'Cunetiu' of doubtful meaning
Lambourn	lamb stream or loam stream
Loddon	possibly from 'lutna' (muddy river)

Some Places

Aldermaston	farm of the (e)aldorman, the king's deputy in Berkshire
Aldworth	an enclosure belonging to Ealda
Arborfield	'feld' is open land, 'arbor' is 'tree', or may refer to an earthwork (except that none is known locally)
Barkham	birch tree meadow
Binfield	open land where 'bent grass' grows
Blewbury	named for the hill fort on the parish boundary. 'Bleo' is variegated – it may have been that the creamy-white chalk soil had a variegated appearance when cultivated.
Bracknell	a spur of land covered with bracken (or possibly a spur of land belonging to someone called Bracca)
Bradfield	'at the broad piece of open land'
Bray	possibly from the French word for mud (a post-Norman conquest naming). Doubt is cast on the suggestion that it is from 'breg' – the brow of a hill. Where's the hill?
Brimpton	an estate associated with Bryni
Bucklebury	Burghild's fortified place (Burghild is a woman's name)
Chalvey	Calve's island (dry land in the middle of a marsh?)
Chieveley	Cifa's 'le(a)h', or woodland clearing (another suggestion associates it with wild chives growing locally)
Cholsey	Ceol's island – a possible reference to Cholsey Hill – dry ground in the middle of a marshy area
Clewer	dwellers on a riverbank (on a cliff?)
Colthrop	Cola's hamlet

Cookham	Cook village? A settlement named for a particular activity?
Crowthorne	appears on Norden's map as a reference to a single (thorn?) tree at the junction of the Bracknell and Wokingham roads
Datchet	the name contains a Celtic word for forest, one of the few Celtic survivors among the area's place names
Donnington	an estate associated with a low hill, or with someone named Dun(n)
Earley	Eagles' wood (or the 'ear' part could possibly relate to gravel)
Easthamstead	homestead by the gate (possibly the gate to the king's forest at Windsor)
Englefield	'open land of the Angles'
Eton	an island farm
Faringdon	fern hill, or possibly settlement of the Farringas
Finchampstead	homestead frequented by finches
Fobney Meadow	Fobba's island (it stands between the main stream and a branch of the Kennet)
Frilsham	Frioel's homestead
Frogmore	possibly the surname of a man concerned with land at Winkfield
Fyfield	an estate rated for tax at five hides. (A hide is a measure of land area, dating from pre-Norman times. In modern terms its value varied from area to area. In Wessex it represented 40–48 acres.)
Grazeley	a badger's wallowing place? (Do badgers wallow?)
Greenham	a green river meadow
Hagbourne	a hedged enclosure by a brook
Hampstead Norris	a homestead, sold to the trustees of John Norreys in 1448
Hurley	a wood or clearing in a recess in the hills
Hurst	a wooded hill
Knowl Hill	if 'knoll' means a hillock, this would make it 'hillock hill'
Lambourn	probably relates to local downland sheep being dipped in a stream or bourne here

Langley	a long clearing at the foot of the Chilterns
Maidenhead	landing place of the maidens. Either a convenient landing place (a new wharf or 'maiden hythe') where it is so well-paved that even maidens can disembark with ease, or somewhere young ladies used to gather. The town actually developed from a Saxon village called South Ellington. There is some suggestion that the great hill at Taplow was known in the Iron Age as 'mai dun'.
Midgham	a riverside meadow infested with midges
Newbury	a new borough (founded on the line of a road between Oxford and Southampton by Ernulf (or Arnulf) de Hesdin, Lord of Ulfritone and an associate of William the Conqueror. He later fell foul of the monarchy and made a hurried departure for the Holy Land, shortly before his lands were 'reallocated'.)
Padworth	an enclosure belonging to Peada
Pangbourne	Stream of Paega's people.
Peasemore	'mere' is pond and 'pise' refers to a plant resembling a pea
Purley	wood or clearing frequented by snipes or bitterns
Remenham	land in a river bend, or water meadow
Ruscombe	Rot's enclosed land
Sandford	a ford on the Old River, a branch of the Loddon
Sandhurst	sandy hill
Shinfield	open land of Sciene's people
Shottesbrooke	Scot's stream or trout stream
Sonning	Sunna's people, the Sunningas. They may have occupied large areas of modern Berkshire, east of Reading, and may have given their name also to Sunninghill and Sunningdale.
South Hill Park	relatively high ground, south of Easthamstead and Bracknell
Spital	site of a leper hospital

Stanford Dingley	a stony ford on the River Pang. A document of 1428 refers to a Robert Dyngley in connection with it.
Stratfield Mortimer	open land traversed by a Roman road (the one from London to Silchester). Was the Mortimer part a later addition by a Norman landowner?
Sulham	'Sulh' is a gulley and 'ham' is an enclosure
Sunninghill and **Sunningdale**	a hill and dale probably associated with a group known as the Sunningas
Thatcham	either 'a thatched village' or 'a river meadow where thatching materials were obtained'
Theale	a plank for crossing a river, or a structure used for holding meetings
Tidmarsh	possibly 'a common marsh'
Tilehurst	a wooded hill where tiles are made
Touchen End	fork of a road, crossroads. Short for Touchen Lane End.
Twyford	double ford. The road from Reading has to cross two branches of the Loddon at this point.
Uffington	the settlement of Offa's descendants – the Uffingas
Ufton Nervet	Uffa's farm, Nervet is thought to be an old Norman surname
Wallingford	the 'Wahl' part reflects some Anglo-Saxon association with a Welshman. Possibly the old ford way of the British or Welsh?
Waltham St Lawrence	open land by the River Swealwe
Warfield	open land associated with a weir, river dam or fishing enclosure in a river
Wargrave	grove by the weirs (or pit)
Welford	a willow ford on the River Lambourn
Whiteknights	possibly after a white knight (Johannes de Arle, or is it Gilbert de Montalieu?) who, legend says, is buried there
White Waltham	The 'white' probably reflects the area's chalky soil. The 'Waltham' is unclear, though could the 'ham' part refer to a farm or homestead?

Whitley	white wood, or a clearing
Windsor	a river bank with a windlass, used for landing goods from barges
Winkfield	Wineca's open land
Winnersh	the components of this name mean 'stubble field' or 'ploughed field', and 'meadow pasture'. It is hard to see how they combine – possibly an estate with an unusually low percentage of arable land to meadow?
Winterbourne	a stream which is dry, except in winter
Wokingham	homestead of the people of Wocc, the Woccingas
Woodley	possibly a meadow by the wood
Woolhampton	an estate associated with someone called Wulflaf
Yattendon	valley of the people of Geat

WHO WAS THAT?

Here's a parlour game for you. See if you can recognise these places in historic Berkshire from their ancient names. Note that, in many cases, this is only one of many possible alternative spellings from antiquity.

Abbandune	Abingdon
Heldremanestune	Aldermaston
Eburghefelde	Arborfield
Bastedene	Basildon
Benetfeld	Binfield
Bleobyrig	Blewbury
Borgefel	Burghfield
Bustleham	Bisham
Cifanlea	Chieveley
Clivore	Clewer
Dideorde	Dedworth
Doudecote	Didcot
Erle	Earley
Estcot	Ascot
Etingeden	Yattendon
Faleslei	Fawley
Hildeslei	Ilsley

Inglefelle	Englefield
Lamb-burnan	Lambourn
Shenyngfelde	Shinfield
Sotesbroc	Shottesbrooke
Soanesfelt	Swallowfield
Taceham	Thatcham
Tuifyrdi	Twyford
Uffentune	Uffington (also called Aescesbyrig)
Ullavintone	Woolhampton
Ulvritone	Newbury
Warwelt	Warfield
Winecan felda	Winkfield
Wuealtham	Waltham

10

THE THAMES

'The Thames is liquid history.' (John Burns MP, 1929)

The Thames flows for 200 miles through the heart of England. It is central to the life of London and has been a route for trade – and war – since Roman times. But it has also shaped the identity of the Thames Valley, of which Berkshire forms a major – perhaps the most important – part. For more than 50 miles and several centuries the Thames formed the northern boundary of historic Berkshire, and even before that it separated the kingdoms of Wessex and Mercia. Many of the old county's most important and historic settlements are clustered along its banks – Windsor, Maidenhead, Reading, Wallingford and Abingdon.

WHAT'S IN A NAME?

According to some authorities, the name 'Thames' is a combination of two rivers – the Isis, which is what they would call the Thames from its source to Dorchester, where it meets the River Thame and becomes the Thame-isis (giving us the Roman or pre-Roman name 'Tamesis'). Others say this is just being pedantic, and that Isis is no more than part of the original Roman name for the whole river.

Equally controversial is the question of where the Thames begins. There appear to be two main claimants. Seven Springs, north of Cirencester, is identified as the starting point of the River Churn, that joins the Thames near Cricklade. Thames Head, north of Kemble, is the other candidate. Thames Head in particular seems, for a good part of the year, to lack a vital ingredient for a river – flowing water.

For what it is worth, the 178-mile Thames long distance footpath starts at Thames Head, as do the waterless indentations of the long-abandoned Thames and Severn Canal. This was opened in 1789 as part of an ambitious (and never very successful) attempt to link

London, Gloucester and Bristol via the River Severn, which ceased operating in the early 1900s and was abandoned in the 1930s.

The river starts to form part of Berkshire's old boundary from near Lechlade. Kelmscott Manor, near Lechlade, became the Thameside home and 'earthly paradise' for William Morris, from 1871 until his death in 1896. Two of the river's most ancient surviving bridges are to be found in this upper part of the Thames.

This brings us on to a further dispute – which one is the oldest? Two of the arches at Radcot date from 1280, while the third is a relative newcomer, having been rebuilt in 1387. Newbridge, between Abingdon and Witney, is the other candidate for the oldest Thames bridge. It dates from the fourteenth century, but challenges Radcot's claims to antiquity among Thames bridges: (a) because Radcot was so heavily damaged and extensively restored during the Wars of the Roses, and (b) because the route of the Thames at Radcot was changed in 1787 and the bridge no longer crosses the main channel of the river. Radcot was also the subject of a civil war skirmish in 1644, as the two sides struggled for control of Oxford.

Whilst on the subject of antiquity, another riverside settlement, Old Windsor, can lay claim to having been a royal residence until

Looking across the Thames at Windsor Castle

usurped by that brash newcomer, New Windsor and its castle, in 1110. Even after Windsor Castle was built, the old manor house remained popular with the monarchy as a hunting lodge, being close to the river and Windsor Forest and, more to the point, rather more comfortable than an austere mediaeval fortress.

Until the eighteenth century, boats had a hard time of it navigating the Thames. Mill owners and fish farmers competed for the use of the river and its water supply. Successive monarchs, and even Magna Carta, tried to legislate against the various abuses practiced by river users, but to no avail. Weirs and eel traps blocked the waterway. Flash locks could lead to dramatic changes in water levels when they were opened to let boats through, which could leave other craft aground for long periods (weeks in the upper reaches of the river). Edward I issued an edict in 1274 for the Thames 'to be so widened that ships and great barges might ascend from London to Oxford, and descend, without hindrance from any weirs; as the Thames was so narrowed in divers places that ships could not pass'.

But his ideal of uninterrupted navigation would be a long time coming. The main transhipment points for river-borne goods in mediaeval Berkshire were Windsor (supplying the castle – the name 'Windsor' means 'windlass by the riverside' – windles-ore in Old English) and Reading (serving the abbey). But for some, the difficulty of getting upstream of Henley was such that they preferred to unload at Henley and risk the muddy and poorly maintained roads for the rest of their journey.

The first modern pound locks on the Thames were built around 1630, at Sandford, Iffley, Culham and the Swift Ditch, Abingdon, but it would be the end of the eighteenth century before anything remotely like proper management existed all along the river. The Thames Commissioners were set up in 1751 to do something about the chaotic traffic on the river, and in 1770 the Corporation of London sought the advice of canal builder James Brindley. He recommended – guess what? – a canal, running from Reading to near Bray, that would cut the journey time from Reading to Bray from three – or even up to fifteen – days, to six hours.

Parliament threw that idea out, but the Commissioners did, at least, install eight further pound locks between Maidenhead and Reading by 1773, with others following in the 1770s and 1780s. Two schemes that were given approval were on the Thames' tributary, the River Kennet – these are detailed in chapter 2.

But Berkshire also had another canal, the Wilts and Berks Canal, which ran from the Thames at Abingdon to the Kennet and Avon Canal at Melksham, with a branch to the Thames and Severn Canal at Cricklade. It was approved in 1795 and completed in 1810. It was not a spectacular success; ground conditions were unsuitable, making running costs very high; a competing railway line was in place from 1841; and the supplies of Somerset coal – its main traffic – ran out. Its use had pretty well ceased by 1901, when the Stanley Aqueduct collapsed, and its formal abandonment in 1914 was a foregone conclusion. Since then, it has suffered many indignities – rubbish dumping, military use for explosives practise, not to mention the small matters of building housing and the M4 motorway over it. Nonetheless, plans are afoot to restore at least parts of it for leisure purposes.

Whilst on the subject of artificial waterways, mention should also be made of the Jubilee River, dug between Maidenhead and Windsor and opened in 2002, to protect this stretch of the Thames from the threat of flooding.

LITERARY ASSOCIATIONS WITH THE THAMES IN BERKSHIRE

Sir Walter Scott used Cumnor and the tragedy of Amy Robsart in his novel *Kenilworth* (Amy Robsart was the first wife of Queen Elizabeth I's favourite, Robert Dudley, who died in suspicious circumstances in 1560, as a result of falling downstairs and breaking her neck at Cumnor Place).

The Beetle and Wedge public house in Moulsford was where H.G. Wells wrote *The History of Mr Polly*.

Kenneth Grahame, author of *The Wind in the Willows*, grew up near the river at Cookham, returned there to live on his retirement and spent the last years of his life in Pangbourne.

Mary Shelley wrote *Frankenstein* in a cottage in Marlow, and Thomas Love Peacock and T.S. Eliot both worked in Marlow at various times.

Jerome K. Jerome's *Three Men in a Boat* was all about a journey along the Thames; it was he who described Abingdon as 'quiet, eminently respectable, clean and desperately dull'.

Not so much a literary figure as a purveyor of popular literature who rose to become First Lord of the Treasury, W.H. Smith owned an Italianate house on the banks of the Thames at Remenham.

THE THAMES AND WAR

As we saw in chapter 8, the Thames was a vital consideration in warfare from the earliest days. Both the Romans and William the Conqueror built fortifications at key points along it (the Romans at Dorchester, and the Normans at Windsor and Wallingford, among

King Charles I

others). Part of the ninth-century Danish invading army arrived in Berkshire by boat up the river, and set up camp just where the coming together of the rivers Thames and Kennet afforded them natural protection from most directions.

As we also saw earlier, during the Civil War control of the Thames crossings was vital to each side's grasp on territory generally. Wallingford Castle dominated a key crossing point on the Thames, and was besieged during both the civil war between Stephen and Matilda, and that between Charles I and Parliament. In the case of Reading, the occupying Royalist forces turned the Thames crossing into an improvised drawbridge, and Charles I himself led a force to try and break the Parliamentary blockade of the bridge.

As recently as the Second World War, defensive preparations against invasion involved the identification of 'stop lines', natural obstacles to movement that could be reinforced by the addition of pill boxes and anti-tank ditches. Very often these stop lines were waterways – the Thames, but in particular, the Kennet and Avon Canal and the River Loddon. A purpose-made anti-tank ditch was dug through the Sulham Gap, from the Kennet and Avon Canal to the Thames at Pangbourne. The line through Berkshire – the GHQ line – was part of the longest and most important of these defences, designed to protect Britain's industrial heartland from the invading enemy. As for the Germans, they found the Thames most useful as a guide to navigation for their bombers on dark nights.

11

THE ROYAL BERKSHIRE REGIMENT

What follows is a brief and highly selective history of the county's own regiment, whose origins go back to 1885. Or 1881. Or was it 1758, or perhaps 1743/44? Did I mention Saxon times?

1885 was the year in which the 'Royal' part of the name was attached to the regiment. Following their sterling service at the Battle of Tofrek in the Sudan, they became the Princess Charlotte of Wales's (Royal Berkshire Regiment). Prior to that, they had simply been (since 1881) the Princess Charlotte of Wales's (Berkshire Regiment), after being formed by the amalgamation of the 66th (Berkshire) Regiment of Foot (raised in 1758), the 49th (Princess Charlotte of Wales's) (Hertfordshire) Regiment of Foot (raised in 1744), the 1st Berkshire Rifle Volunteer Corps (formed in 1859) and the Berkshire Militia (1757 or very much earlier). All clear so far? Me neither. Let's unpick it a little.

Some of the earliest origins of the Berkshire Regiment go back to one Edward Trelawny, a Cornishman, Governor of Jamaica from 1738, and a man with no military background whatsoever (his father was Bishop of Winchester). However, it did not take a military genius to work out that the arrangements for the defence of Jamaica were a shambles, with eight independent companies of troops, and he began to lobby the government in London for them to be properly coordinated.

The Secretary of State was none too keen on the idea (and, in particular, the cost involved) and Trelawny had to lobby until 1743 before he got his consent to form what became (in 1744) the 49th. His problems as colonel of the new regiment were largely non-military – they included having little military activity to keep the troops occupied; endemic, and often fatal, fever; and few leisure time activities that did not involve excessive drinking and/or 'the dubious delights of the negro towns' (as one regimental historian put it).

At first they were limited to light home duties – intimidating the local population and scrapping with the odd raiding pirate, while the Royal Navy provided the bulk of the island's defences. It was not until 1764 that the regiment got its first overseas posting – to Ireland.

The outbreak of the American Revolutionary War in 1775 saw the regiment landing in Boston, and fighting on such unlikely battlefields as the Bronx, Brooklyn and Long Island. When the French entered the war on the side of the colonists in 1778, the 49th were part of a British force that invaded the French island of St Lucia. A powerful French fleet soon arrived carrying 9,000 soldiers, and the 49th's part in driving them off earned them their first battle honour.

By 1792 they were posted to French St Domingo, where they struggled to maintain law and order in a situation of total chaos

Lord Nelson

and where fever decimated them. By the time they were posted to England for the first time, in 1796, they numbered less than 150 sick and exhausted men. They were quartered in Watford, at that time having no link with the royal county. Rested and reinforced, they were eventually ready to help face the threat of Napoleon and his allies. In 1801 they sailed to Copenhagen, with a fleet which had a young Nelson as its second in command, to attack the Danish fleet. The 49th's presence was largely ornamental in what was essentially a naval battle – one which Nelson won. Service in Canada followed, at the end of which, in 1815, 115 members of the regiment took their discharge in Canada and became settlers there.

Meanwhile, a new regiment, the 66th, was being formed in 1758, during the Seven Years' War. One of its early overseas postings was that dreaded island of St Domingo again, where, in a single year, fever took fifteen officers and 691 soldiers, as they struggled to put down a rebellion by the black population. By the time they left in 1798, the 66th numbered just eighty-six men.

In 1816, the 66th were ordered to St Helena, the island to which Napoleon had been exiled. When Napoleon died in 1821, members of the 66th were some of his pall bearers. After a period of service in Canada, the regiment returned to England, at the start of 'forty years going the rather dull round of peacetime stations' (the words of that regimental historian again).

By 1815 the 49th were back in England, and were detailed to guard members of the Royal Family at their favoured seaside resort, Weymouth. Their smart new uniforms so impressed the young Princess Charlotte that she asked for the 49th to become 'her' regiment. So, in 1816 the 49th became Princess Charlotte of Wales's Regiment. (As a footnote to history, Princess Charlotte was the only child of George IV. She died in 1817, after giving birth to a stillborn child. Had either lived, we might never have had a Queen Victoria.)

The regiment saw service in China and the Crimean War (the latter notable for some hand-to-hand fighting outside Sebastopol, where a Lieutenant Conolly wielded a heavy brass-bound telescope in lieu of a bayonet, winning himself a Victoria Cross, and paving the way for his promotion to lieutenant colonel in the Coldstream Guards in the process).

By the 1870s moves were afoot to bring the 49th and the 66th together. In 1878 a joint regimental depot, the Brock Barracks on Reading's Oxford Road, was opened.

The 1880s saw the Afghan wars and the Battle of Maiwand, described elsewhere in the book, and commemorated in the Forbury

Gardens. It was the last glorious stand of the 66th as a separate regiment. On 1 July 1881, the two regiments became the 1st and 2nd battalions of the Berkshire Regiment (Princess Charlotte of Wales's). (The 49th had previously been associated with Hertfordshire, for some reason.) As we saw, the Sudan campaign and the Battle of Tofrek saw them add the title 'Royal' to their name. The Battle of Ginnis, in the Sudan in 1885, also marked the last time the regiment fought in a scarlet uniform, as opposed to khaki.

The 1st Battalion was performing royal guarding duties at Osborne House when the Boer War got under way. The commanding officer mentioned to Her Majesty that his greatest wish was to go out to South Africa on active service. He was regally, but sharply, reminded that guarding the royal person was the highest duty to which he, or any soldier, could aspire. As for the 2nd Battalion, they saw active service helping the civil authorities subdue serious rioting in Newlyn, Cornwall, in 1896 (before you ask, it was all to do with unloading fishing boats on a Sunday ...).

The Berkshire Militia had more ancient origins than any other part of the newly formed regiment. It is thought that such forces had been convened periodically since Saxon times, though early records are understandably sketchy. Certainly Berkshire raised militias in 1377, 1378, 1380 (danger of French invasion) and when the Armada threatened in 1588.

The county militias were reactivated in 1757 to protect the country from invasion during the Seven Years' War. Each county had a quota of men to fill, by ballot if necessary, though the better off whose name came out of the hat could pay for someone else to serve their turn. This latter practice hit mainstream army recruiting, because substituting for someone in the militia soon became better paid than serving in your own right in the regular army. It was disbanded after the war but called out again for the American Revolution in 1777, and once more to respond to the threat of Napoleon between 1792 and 1816.

The coming war with Russia led to yet another reincarnation in 1852. By then, all that remained of the militia's equipment from 1816 was a dozen ancient and rusty flintlocks and two drums (one broken). However, they sorted themselves out sufficiently to serve overseas (in Corfu) in 1855, before being swept into the Berkshire Regiment in the army reforms of 1881.

There were even volunteer forces (a kind of Home Guard) raised from the late eighteenth century onwards, though the governments of the day were sometimes reticent about arming what was often a fractious civil population. Six companies were raised in Berkshire, and some of them went on to serve with distinction in South Africa during the Boer War.

The Royal Berkshires were engaged in the First World War almost from day one (to be precise, they were in France from day nine, and in action ten days after that). Like so much of the 'old' British Army, they suffered huge casualties at the First Battle of Ypres, and after a year of the war, few of the original troops remained. On the first day of the Somme offensive alone (1 July 1916) they lost twenty

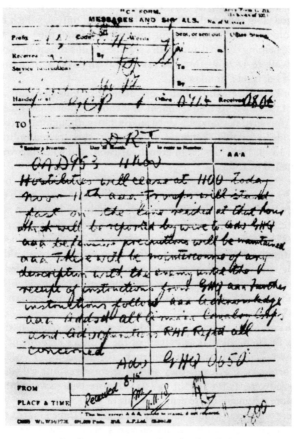

A telegram announcing the Armistice

officers and 437 other ranks. They were, nonetheless, engaged in virtually every major action on the Western Front, and the list of their battle honours reads like a history of that part of the Great War. Their last action was fought in October 1918, just days before the Armistice. In addition, virtually every member of the Territorial battalion volunteered to extend their home defence remit, to serve overseas. The regiment came out of the Great War with fifty-five battle honours, and a death toll of 6,688 men of all ranks.

Come the start of the Second World War and the regiment was partly in Britain and partly in India. The British part headed off to France in September 1939, and what was left of it came back, via Dunkirk, the following May. It later served in India, fighting what Lieutenant General Sir Brian Horrocks described as 'one of the turning points of the war', to stand alongside Alamein and Stalingrad. This was the 1944 battle for Kohima in Assam, on the border with Burma (for the Japanese, their gateway to India). The Berkshires helped relieve the exhausted troops that had been defending this vital hill village, and for weeks held off larger Japanese forces, fighting at the closest quarters in appalling conditions, and with food, water and sleep in desperately short supply. Kohima was the high point of the Japanese advance into Asia, and the coming of the monsoon season was followed by the announcement of their retreat, leaving behind thousands of their dead.

The regiment also served in other Second World War theatres, such as Egypt, Italy, and in Normandy from D-Day and beyond. After the war, a reduction in the size of the armed forces led to the regiment's amalgamation into the Duke of Edinburgh's Royal Regiment (Berkshire and Wiltshire) in 1959.

12

BERKSHIRE TAKES ON HITLER

In this chapter we look at some of the ways in which the Second World War impacted on the people of Berkshire.

EVACUEES

Perhaps the first big impact of the war on Berkshire was the massive influx of evacuees that occurred in September 1939. Reading's position was ambivalent; on the one hand, it was far enough from London to be considered a safe place to send evacuees – a 'reception area'. On the other, it had enough targets, in the way of railway junctions, manufacturing industry and government offices, to make it likely that the town would receive the unwelcome attentions of the Luftwaffe in its own right. It was, for example, the Southern Region Civil Defence Headquarters, and wartime home to several government departments, including the BBC's Monitoring Service for the gathering of enemy intelligence (still present, in Caversham Park). Museums stored some of their precious exhibits in the Knowl Hill chalk mines. Slough was also a big industrial area, and even closer to London and the main centre of bombing.

Nonetheless, Reading alone received around 25,000 children in the first week of September and, in total, Berkshire was asked to play host to 46,722 evacuees, almost double the number originally expected. What with evacuees, war workers and others, Reading became so overpopulated that by 1941 it was declared a 'closed town' and further movement there was banned. Meanwhile, Wokingham and its rural district got 8,300, and in Windsor, some 5,000 evacuees had been housed by January 1941, but more than 100 were still camped out in a hall awaiting a new home.

Royal Berkshire also had a more select class of evacuee; several exiled royals – Queen Wilhelmina of Holland, King Haakon of Norway, King Peter of Yugoslavia and King Zog of Albania – found a wartime home in the county.

The local press swiftly switched into wartime propaganda mode, painting a picture of delirious happiness on the part of evacuees and hosts alike:

> Newbury people have given the little Londoners and their mothers a hospitable welcome, and the evacuees, for their part have taken immediately to their warm-hearted hosts ... Already these pale-faced Londoners are showing the benefits of walks in the common, bathing in the river and cricket and football in the parks.

The reality was a much more mixed picture. Whilst many did undoubtedly have a happy relationship (or at least manage to rub along without major conflict), many tensions could threaten the relationship. For the evacuees there was homesickness and the challenge of an unfamiliar environment. A proportion of the hosts would have been very unwilling recipients of their new charges, some of them having made more or less ingenious efforts to evade the billeting order. Then there were the cultural differences between hosts and guests.

The evacuees have tended in the past to be portrayed as urban working-class children from a poverty-stricken background, clashing with their more rural, affluent, middle-class (and, by implication, civilised) hosts. But more recent research at Reading University has suggested that the picture is much more complex, with at least as many middle-class children having difficulty coping with their working-class foster homes. There were also practical problems, like the overcrowding of local schools – for example, Bradfield School saw its school roll rise from 110 to 184 virtually overnight, and a shift system for teaching had to be introduced to cope with them.

There were also practical problems: children arriving with barely more than the clothes they stood up in; babies with no prams and older children with unwelcome visitors (in their hair); the Billeting Officer at Hungerford reported that forty of the 170 children she had been asked to rehouse were verminous, and sales of disinfectant and nit powder in some areas soon left the chemists' shelves bare.

Whatever the causes, significant numbers of evacuees soon returned to their urban homes, especially when the anticipated bombing raids failed at first to materialise. In Slough, one evacuee in ten left during the first week, and a quarter had returned home by the end of September 1939. Slough apparently had the additional problem that evacuees thought it too close to London and therefore not safe enough. At the same time, there were genuine success stories, like the two Reading sisters who took on the care of no less than nineteen evacuee babies and still found time to make a small mountain of handicrafts for the war effort.

In addition to evacuated children, there were war workers and members of the armed forces to be billeted, sick and disabled evacuees and – once the bombing started in earnest – unofficial evacuees, looking to escape the Blitz. Riverside locations, like Purley-on-Thames, became particularly attractive to anyone who could get access to a holiday home along the Thames or even a habitable boat. Even the grandstand at Ascot racecourse was used as a temporary home for some of the troops evacuated from Dunkirk.

On a lighter note, army billeting officers went to Sandhurst, looking for places to billet members of the Black Watch. One of the places they were offered was a room above a garage, the only access to which was via a ladder. Given that the Black Watch uniform included a kilt, and that there were young ladies on the site, it was felt that this might give the ladies more information than they required as to what was worn under the kilt. The offer was declined.

THE BLITZ

Considering how close parts of Berkshire are to London, and the number of potentially interesting targets it had to offer (everything from Windsor Castle and the Royal Family, to vital railway junctions and manufacturing centres), Berkshire got off relatively lightly in the Blitz, in terms of damage. Having said that, 1,595 bombs fell on Berkshire between July 1940 and May 1941 alone.

Perhaps the single worst raid came on the afternoon of Wednesday 10 February 1943, when a single low-flying Dornier bomber swept over the centre of Reading, machine gunning the streets as it went and dropping a string of bombs across the heart of the town. They hit a furniture repository, the back of Wellsteed's department store and did extensive damage to the Town Hall and the neighbouring church. In all of these areas, it was a blessing that it was early closing day and the town was less crowded than it would normally have been.

But the real damage, in terms of loss of life, was done in the nearby People's Restaurant. In total, forty-one people were killed in the raid, forty-nine seriously injured and 104 slightly injured. At the time, wartime censorship meant that the public could learn little or nothing about it from the newspapers. Reports in the next edition of the *Berkshire Chronicle* merely spoke of a hit-and-run raid on a 'home counties town'. Not until many weeks later would they be able to read that the target had been Reading, though most of the readership probably guessed.

Reading also suffered other, lesser raids, including the demolition of several houses in November 1940. It took until 1944 for the newspaper to reveal that what their original report referred to as 'considerable damage to working class property in a Home Counties town' had actually taken place in Reading's Cardiff Road.

On the same day as Reading's big raid, another bomber attacked the centre of Newbury, destroying St John's Church, Newbury Senior Council School and St Bartholomew's almshouses, among other buildings, and killing fifteen people. It is thought both bombers were themselves shot down before reaching the coast.

Windsor and Maidenhead both suffered damage from raids, as well as finding themselves just within the range of the V1 flying bombs. There were a total of 202 V1 alerts, and several fell in the areas around Windsor, causing some deaths and many casualties. One flying bomb that fell in Cookham Road, Maidenhead, caused sixty-two injuries. It is estimated that around 1,000 properties in Windsor and its surrounding areas suffered some degree of bomb damage. The emergency services were kept busy, but not just with local problems – Windsor firemen also helped to fight air raid blazes in Bristol, Liverpool and Manchester. In total, 1,723 bombs fell on Berkshire, outside Reading, with the eastern end of the county getting a larger share of them.

In Slough, the trading estate had its own unusual means of hiding their property from the bombers. They burned lots of waste materials that concealed their factories beneath a thick pall of oily smoke that was probably as threatening to people's health as any bombing raid. Slough seemed to get off relatively lightly – perhaps their smokescreen worked? One bomb that fell on the High Duty Alloys factory created 'a river of molten metal', and only quick thinking on the part of the employees prevented it burning the premises down.

THE WAR IN THE AIR

The war history of Woodley Airfield is dealt with in the transport chapter, but Woodley was not Berkshire's only wartime airfield. Among the others, White Waltham was opened in 1935 by de Havilland as a flying school. During the Second World War it was commandeered as the headquarters of the Air Transport Auxiliary. This organisation transported new, damaged and repaired planes between the manufacturers and the front line airfields, as well as chauffeuring service personnel on urgent missions, and running air ambulances.

In the course of the war they delivered over 308,000 planes of 130 different types, from Spitfires to Lancaster bombers. Their selection of pilots was based purely on whether they could do the job. Age, short-sightedness or minor disabilities such as missing limbs were no impediment; good heavens, they even let women fly their planes! By the end of the war, not only were the women entrusted with virtually every type of plane, they were almost unique at the time in receiving equal pay to their male counterparts. Since the war, White Waltham has mainly been used for private flying, though some RAF flying continued there until 1973.

Aldermaston Airfield was originally opened for the RAF in 1942, but was shortly afterwards handed over to troop-carrying units of the United States air force. Some fifty-two troop carrying gliders were towed from the site on D-Day, and the base also contributed to the tragic raid on Arnhem (many more of the Arnhem troops flew from Membury). After the war Aldermaston briefly became a civil airfield until, in 1950, the site was taken over by the Atomic Weapons Research Establishment and helped to develop the first British nuclear bomb, exploded at the Monte Bello Islands, Australia, in 1952.

Greenham Common (which had the longest runway in Europe) was used by USAAF during the war; a total of thirty-three glider crews flying from there were killed. It was decommissioned in 1946 and fell into disuse until 1950. The whole site was then redeveloped as a major USAAF airbase (and a mecca for peace campaigners) during the Cold War. Cruise missiles operated from there from 1983. USAAF left in 1992 and the site was put up for sale the following year.

Bombers flew from Abingdon, Harwell and Hampstead Norreys; improbably, some sixty-five Wellington bombers were assembled in a hangar at Smith's Lawn, in Windsor Great Park (this was presumably the same landing strip used before the war by the King's Flight and King George V). Theale had its own training field, using

Tiger Moth biplanes. It used to suffer badly from waterlogging and is now totally under water since they extracted the gravel from it. There were also glider airfields at Harwell and Membury, and at least a dozen other airfields, used variously for training, emergency landings, as decoy airfields or for 'other uses', such as storage or training air traffic controllers.

Berkshire even had a part to play in the war on the water. Local boat owners formed themselves into an Upper Thames patrol, ceaselessly guarding against enemy incursions in their armed cabin cruisers.

WAR MUNITIONS

Not for nothing did the Slough Trading Estate try to hide itself from prying German eyes. Like just about every other part of the economy, it had been placed on a war footing and was making war materials, including Spitfires and incendiary bombs. Hurricane fighters, designed by a Windsor man, Sydney Camm, were being built at the Hawker factory in Langley, and parts of Spitfires were being assembled all over the place, including the Vincent motor works in central Reading. These would be collected at dead of night by RAF transporters and shipped off to secret destinations for assembly into complete planes.

Bofors ack-ack guns were built in another secret factory, hidden in the Tubney Wood, near the Oxfordshire border.

Elliott's gave up making furniture, and started building Horsa gliders and components for other aircraft, and the Newbury Diesel Company made ships' engines. But one of Newbury's most striking contributions to the war effort was the rail depot that was established on the racecourse. After horse racing finished in September 1941, they covered the course in coconut matting and laid some 37 miles of railway track over it. A huge depot was developed, able to supply anything from petrol to bailey bridges. In the run-up to D-Day almost 7,000 people worked there, meeting the food and many of the other day-to-day requirements of up to 125,000 troops.

With petrol in short supply and coastal shipping largely ruled out by the U-boats, the railways became vital wartime arteries for moving people and materials around the country. Anticipating that lines could be put out of use by air raids, the authorities looked for alternative routes between key areas. One of these was the link between the industrial Midlands and the south coast ports, and the alternative they looked at was the line between Didcot, Newbury and Southampton. It was a little-used single track country route, and major engineering works were needed to make it capable of taking wartime levels of traffic. This included upgrading a large section of it to twin tracks and providing long passing loops on the rest, to enable heavy goods trains to use it. For the duration of the war it was used to absolutely full capacity and above, with trains queuing up to use it. Civilian patronage never recovered after the war, though, and the line was gradually run down, with the last passenger services ceasing in 1962 and complete closure in 1964.

BLACKOUT

The other wartime measure that had a huge and immediate impact on everyone in Berkshire was the blackout. It was introduced two days before the official declaration of war and people were given just one day to comply with its daunting requirements. With no light from houses or shops, no street lights, only heavily dimmed torches allowed and the headlights on vehicles reduced to feeble slots, the night-time world became a dark and dangerous place, with deaths from road accidents rising to roughly double the peacetime level. As the *British Medical Journal* put it, the Luftwaffe were killing 600 British civilians a month, without even taking to the air.

In Reading's Broad Street, two women were knocked down and killed by a bus. The baby they had in a pram was hurled into the air but was miraculously caught, unharmed, by its grandfather, despite the lack of visibility.

Vehicles had their running boards and other extremities painted white in an effort to make them more visible in the dark, and the authorities painted white lines down the middle of roads, to enable drivers to stay on the correct side of the road. One Wokingham motorist mistook the kerb for the white line and drove merrily along the pavement, until he crashed into an unexpected pillar box and then a tree. In Reading, an army lorry whose driver thought he was bowling along the Oxford Road was in fact on a parallel street, and suddenly came upon a brick wall where the road should have been. In the accident which followed, two of his passengers were killed and another thirteen injured.

Luminous armbands and wearing or carrying something white were all proposed. If all else failed, gentlemen could leave their shirt tails hanging out. There were even dangers in bumping into other pedestrians – there was at least one case of someone being killed in such a collision.

A small army of Air Raid Wardens were on hand to enforce the blackout regulations, and some did so with a zeal that sounds excessive to us today. There were prosecutions in Berkshire for people striking matches in the street, for sucking their cigarette too vigorously, causing it to glow, and, for one lady, allowing the pilot light of her electric iron to wink near an unshielded window. Public telephone boxes – vital for reporting emergencies in the days before mobile phones or even widespread possession of landlines – were also unlit, and therefore virtually unusable at night, as a reporter from the *Slough Observer* was to discover when he decided to test out the emergency services telephone line.

The use of public transport was also fraught with difficulty. When a bus came, there was no illuminated sign to tell you which service it was. Once on board, the conductor could not see to collect your fares, and Reading Transport reported an increase in the number of dud foreign coins being passed. In the dark, you were unable to see where you were, and thus where you needed to get off. Having reached what you thought was your destination, it was difficult to tell – especially with the silent-running trolley buses – whether the bus had come to a standstill. Many a passenger went flying from getting off too soon. Similarly, on the railways passengers were warned to make sure they were stopped in a station, next to a platform, before alighting. Two passengers stepped mistakenly out of their carriages only to disappear, respectively, off a viaduct into a river and off a bridge, with only the ground to break his fall.

But at least there was a bright side to the blackout for some – if such a thing is not a contradiction in terms. The British Astronomical Association reported that the conditions for stargazing were the best they had seen in twenty-five years, and the Methodist churches in Newbury were able to organise a moonlight ramble for their parishioners. It was also good for the sales of carrots. The authorities found that the 'Dig for Victory' campaign had left them with a surplus of 100,000 tons of carrots and, as part of the campaign to get them eaten, they put it about that the carotene in carrots was the secret to RAF pilots' keen night vision, that enabled them to see the Luftwaffe in the dark. It was a fiction, of course, designed to conceal the fact that the RAF had airborne radar, but it got people munching to improve their ability to see in the blackout.

As the end of the war approached and the danger of air raids receded, the authorities were allowed to restore street lighting. In

Newbury, Reading and no doubt elsewhere, crowds gathered in the streets to witness this new fairyland. Small children had never known a world with lit streets. In Newbury's case this consisted of just twenty-four 100 watt bulbs, about 90 yards apart and just about bright enough to read a newspaper by, if you stood directly underneath. Hungerford came to be known as probably the best lit town of its size, its council having installed new concrete lamp posts just before the easing of the blackout regulations.

HOLIDAYS AT HOME

With seaside beaches mined and barbed wired against invasion, and non-essential travel discouraged, people were asked to have holidays at home. Local authorities tried to put on a range of leisure type activities that would replace real holidays, but these were all too often high-minded attempts to put on what the councillors thought people ought to have, rather than what they would actually enjoy. Some Berkshire authorities at least had the advantage of the Thames as a basis for water-related fun. In Windsor, the Home Park was filled with fancy dress contests, tennis tournaments, horticultural shows and brass band concerts. They were judged a relative failure; as one Windsor councillor sourly put it: 'you do not get a holiday by staying at home'.

In Reading, the council lifted its long-standing ban on organised sports in their parks on Sundays, and drew up a packed programme of sports, competitions and worthy activities, such as folk dancing. A touch of the exotic was introduced by having Chinese dragon boats on their part of the Thames. But the main activity they promoted seemed to be committee meetings, setting up four main committees and innumerable sub-committees to coordinate it all. Surely the most ill-advised initiative must have been the 'Holidays at School' programme, in which schools were kept open and staffed during the summer holidays to give the children extra tuition. The pupils were notable by their almost total absence.

13

INDUSTRIAL BERKSHIRE

In this chapter we look at some of the industries that have contributed to Berkshire's prosperity over the years.

CLOTH AND CLOTHING

For centuries, spinning, weaving and the making of clothes was one of Berkshire's main industries. There is some evidence to suggest that the industry was established as early as the reign of Henry I in the twelfth century, and an Act of 1258 prohibited the export of British wool and sought to promote cloth making in England. Before that, raw bales of British wool were often exported, for use by continental weavers, though there is evidence of a clothing industry in Reading from as early as 1253. At its height (during the reign of the Tudors) the industry was said to support half the local population. At that time:

> There were few or no beggars at all; poor people who God had blessed with most children did by means of this occupation so order them that when they were come to five or seven years of age they were able to get their own bread.

The downland sheep produced a particularly fine grade of wool, though the cloth the Berkshire weavers produced from it was rather coarse and heavy, compared with that of their Flemish counterparts. This was, to some extent, addressed during the reign of Edward III, when unrest on the Continent brought Flemish émigrés into Berkshire. Newbury and Reading were the two big centres of the industry, though there were individual manufacturers scattered around the county.

Clothing entrepreneurs could become exceedingly wealthy. One of the best known during Henry VII's and VIII's time was one John

Winchcombe, better known as Jack of Newbury. He was apprenticed to a clothing manufacturer in Newbury and, when his master died somewhat prematurely, he did his career prospects no harm at all by marrying his master's widow. The business flourished under his management, and he was able to live royally in a grand house (which still exists) in Northbrook Street where he was referred to as 'the richest clothier England ever beheld'.

At his own expense he supplied 100 troops to fight for the king at the Battle of Flodden. He, and they, so distinguished themselves that Henry VII offered him a knighthood (which he refused). He did, however, become an MP, was a great benefactor to Newbury and had a novel written about his exploits, by Thomas Deloney. It was he who funded the building of Newbury's 'wool church', St Nicholas's, which was completed by his son.

Another very successful Newbury clothier was Thomas Dolman. He spent £10,000 in 1581 building Shaw House, then just outside the town, in which he entertained Queen Elizabeth I in 1592.

John Kendrick of Reading was one of the most prosperous of the clothiers of the early seventeenth century. He left money in his will to build the Oracle, a workplace for Reading's destitute clothing workers, roughly on the site of the current Oracle Shopping Centre. His good intentions backfired, due to mismanagement of his inheritance by members of the Corporation. They used it to undercut the competition for clothing orders, and in an industry that was, by then, starting to decline, his misapplied benevolence resulted in more destitution, rather than less.

What the Corporation began, the Civil War accelerated, with its occupations and the taxing of Reading. As we saw, the town's supplies of wool bales were even used to help build the walls that fortified the besieged town. The industry limped on into the eighteenth century, albeit with ever fewer employees and ever lower pay. The decline of the Berkshire woollen industry had a number of causes – the growth of continental competition, the dislocation caused by wars and the burden of taxation on exports. But the major reason may have been their failure to keep up with changing fashions.

By 1716 and for a century afterwards the inmates of the Oracle were engaged in spinning coarse flax, used for making sailcloth, among other products. No doubt they supplied the nearby sail making factory of Musgrave Lamb in Katesgrove Lane, whose products were widely ordered by the governments of the day. Perhaps parts of Nelson's fleet at Trafalgar were propelled by sails made in Reading?

In something of a last hurrah for the local clothing industry, Greenham clothier, John Coxeter, placed a 100 guinea wager in 1811. He bet that he could shear sheep in the morning, have their wool spun and woven into cloth and have that cloth made into clothing before the sun set that same day. He succeeded, as an audience of 5,000 were able to testify, and his Newbury coat was exhibited at the Great Exhibition of 1851.

BRICKS, TILES AND POTS

Much of Berkshire sits on deposits of clay suitable for making pots and building materials, and brickworks have been a significant employer throughout the county since at least the fourteenth century. The section of this book on Slough records the contribution their kilns made to some notable buildings, and one of the earliest recorded orders for the Reading brick maker, William Brockman, was to supply 200,000 serviceable bricks and '20,000 large and serviceable tiles at 12*s* 6*d* per thousand' to build Reading's original Oracle in 1627/28.

Many kilns were in operation in Reading by the late 1700s, most of them in the Katesgrove and Coley areas. The growth of Reading during the Victorian years spurred on the development of new kilns at Kentwood, Norcot and Prospect Park. Bricks almost came to be the fourth 'B' of Victorian Reading's industrial growth, alongside beer, biscuits and bulbs. There was a similar story to the west, with the Pinewood Estate Brick and Tile Works at Hermitage opening in 1891 as one of the most substantial manufacturers in the Newbury area.

Berkshire bricks and tiles are to be found in many important buildings. Eton, Harrow and the Royal Holloway Colleges all used bricks from Thomas Lawrence & Sons at Swinley; Eastheath Works at Wokingham produced facing bricks for Westminster Cathedral; Tilehurst Potteries provided roofs for the prime minister's country house, Chequers, the Middle Temple of the London Law Courts and Sussex College of Cambridge University; and handmade bricks from Warfield were used for restoration work at 10 Downing Street, Windsor Castle and Hampton Court.

The business was still important in the inter-war years. Tilehurst Potteries alone were still turning out some 20 million tiles a year, not to mention flower pots (bearing the royal crest) for Kew Gardens and the London Royal Parks. But in the booming post-war years, it proved difficult to recruit staff to this strenuous and dirty work. That, and the builders' preference for cement tiles, did for the Tilehurst company in the 1960s. Berkshire's last operating brickworks, Star Works at Knowl Hill, closed in 1992.

BREWING

The Berkshire Downs produced a large quantity of high grade barley, ideal for producing malt, the raw material for beer, and the county's rivers and canals could deliver it to London, Bristol and other major markets. Small wonder, then, that malting and brewing became one of Berkshire's staple industries from the eighteenth century.

Each town had a proliferation of brewers, large and small. As at 1864, Reading had no less than fourteen, Newbury nine, Abingdon five, Windsor, Maidenhead, Wantage and Hungerford three each, and so on, with even tiny settlements like Speen, Letcombe Bassett and Chieveley each having their own brewery. But, takeovers and closures took their toll, and names that would have been dear to the hearts of earlier generations of drinkers disappeared – like the Wallingford Brewery Company; Nicholson's at Maidenhead; Neville Read & Co. at Windsor and the South Berkshire Brewery at Newbury. By 1939 the number of Berkshire breweries had shrunk to eight and, by 2000 just two – Courage's (formerly Simonds) at Reading and Morland at Abingdon. Even those two have since quit Berkshire, as we shall see.

One of the most prominent of the county's early brewers was Reading's William Simonds, who was able to start the business, partly by courtesy of an inheritance and partly as a result of the dowry he got from marrying the daughter of a brewer from Basingstoke. William – or rather the Simonds Company – later showed their gratitude to William's father-in-law by taking over his company. Simonds brewery opened in 1785 on the site of what is today Reading's Oracle shopping centre, and in 1797 he even installed the wonder of the age, a Boulton and Watt steam engine.

The business passed to his son, Blackall Simonds, who was noted for his robust business methods. He once threatened to resolve a dispute by fighting a duel with a business rival and, as an active Tory politician, was accused of making 'practical appeals' to voters (or, as we would say, bribing them). He also used his enthusiasm for hunting as an opportunity to look for suitable pub sites as he galloped around the county.

By 1839, Simonds was the largest Reading brewer. Among their other achievements, they developed a new type of beer – pale ale – that would survive the journey to Australia by sailing ship; they had lucrative contracts with the army; and they would later become purveyors of beer to the travelling public in railway canteens and on a variety of seaside piers. Over the years they took over many local breweries, but in 1960 they were themselves swallowed up by the

Courage empire, who first moved the company from the town centre to Worton Grange on the southern tip of Reading, near the M4, and then severed the company's links with the town entirely.

Morland at Abingdon has an even longer pedigree. They first started brewing ale in 1711 at West Ilsley, and their products were soon in demand in London drinking places. Over the years they grew and swallowed up smaller concerns, including a good many smaller Berkshire breweries. In the 1860s this included the Abbey Brewery at Abingdon and, by the 1880s, Morland had moved their main operation to the town.

They continued to grow under the acute management of one Thomas Scurray, even branching out into soft drinks in 1910. They further cemented their links with Abingdon in 1979 by producing what has become their most famous product – a beer called 'Old Speckled Hen'. This commemorated the fiftieth anniversary of the MG Car Company's move to Abingdon, and the 'hen' in question was in fact a car – a lightweight model with a fabric-covered body, finished in an unusual speckled paint job. This was said to be due to them parking it near the paint shop, where it had got spattered. The car had travelled to Abingdon with the company in 1929, and had become well-known around the town as the 'Ould Speckl'd Un' (which got translated into 'speckled hen').

In 1999, they too fell victim to takeover. They were bought out by the Suffolk brewers, Greene King, who closed down the Abingdon plant the following year and moved all production to their Bury St Edmunds factory, from whence Old Speckled Hen and their other beers now come.

But what about the retail end of the brewing business? For many communities that meant the beer shop, a form of public house that could only sell beer, not wine or spirits. They were brought into existence by the Beer Act of 1830. This was passed by a government that was worried about the increased consumption of gin, resulting from a recent reduction in the excise duty on spirits. Its aim was to make beer more readily available, in the hope that it would reduce gin consumption. (Beer was considered a healthier and more nutritious alternative – it was also the safest thing to drink at a time when few people had access to a safe supply of drinking water.)

Hundreds of beer shops opened across Berkshire (nationally, 45,500 such establishments were licensed by 1841). The Act also repealed all duties on strong ale and cider – effectively cutting its price by 20 per cent. Whilst it did wonders for the sale of beer and cider, the effect of the Act on gin consumption was far less marked.

Brewers in Berkshire, and elsewhere, loved this new Act. They employed travelling salesmen to tour the county, encouraging people to turn a room in their home into a beer house. Some would even pay the two guinea (£2 10*d*) license fee that was the only entry requirement, or would lend the would-be landlord the cost of setting up in business, provided he bought his beer from them.

Communities like Purley and Cippenham, which had been without a public house for a century, now had a beer house in their midst. William IV and the Duke of Wellington (respectively the monarch and the prime minister under whom the legislation was enacted) became two of the most popular pub names.

Simonds actually bought more than forty properties in anticipation of the new legislation and opened them as beer houses the minute it became law. The effects of the Act on the nation's health may have been questionable, but it is thought to have had a positive impact on revolutionary tendencies in troubled times, in that many would-be protestors were too sozzled to march on the seats of power!

BISCUITS: HUNTLEY & PALMERS

Baking biscuits started out as a sideline for the Huntley family. Thomas Huntley was a schoolteacher from Gloucestershire and his wife, Hannah, started baking biscuits and selling them to passing stagecoach passengers. They moved to Reading in about 1811, and their son Joseph opened a biscuit and confectionery shop on London Street in 1822. Another member of the family went to work for a nearby firm making tinplate boxes, and they hit on the idea of selling their biscuits in these, as a means of keeping them fresh. As the business grew, so Thomas' health deteriorated. He started to look for a business partner to share the burden and (so company legend has it) a chance meeting outside the Crown Hotel brought him into contact with George Palmer. The Huntley & Palmers partnership was born in 1841, at which time the business was valued at just over £1,000.

Palmer soon emerged as the driving force of the partnership, introducing all sorts of automated machinery to the biscuit-making process, which he got a local maker of agricultural machinery to manufacture. These experiments were not always successful – they often broke down, and one of his new ovens blew up, nearly killing the staff working nearby, but the firm flourished. They started exporting from 1844, exhibited their wares at the Great Exhibition of 1851, and soon every first-class passenger on the Great Western Railway out of Paddington was issued with a small packet of biscuits to fortify them on their journey (GWR did not provide restaurant cars until the 1890s).

By 1860 they were the greatest biscuit manufacturer in the land, and there seemed to be no corner of the world too obscure for their products to reach. Henry Stanley took them as gifts for the natives when he went looking for Dr Livingstone; the fanatical Sudanese followers of the Mahdi fought in the Battle of Omdurman with sword scabbards decorated with cut-out pieces of tinplate from biscuit tins; and, when a party landed on the uninhabited island of Juan Fernandez in the Pacific (thought to be the model for *Robinson Crusoe*'s castaway island), the only evidence of civilisation they found was a Huntley & Palmers biscuit tin. In 1904, tins were found in Lhasa, Tibet, a city forbidden to westerners; the tins were used as ballot boxes in Switzerland; protective bible stores in Uganda (to stop them being eaten by white ants); and as status symbols by Mongolian chiefs.

Huntley & Palmers became the world's greatest biscuit manufacturer and Reading's largest employer. More than 7,000 people worked for them by the early twentieth century. But, thereafter, the firm began a decline – their manufacturing equipment and business methods were out of date, many new rivals emerged and the world wars disrupted their export markets. They merged with Peek Frean in 1920 to form the Associated Biscuit Manufacturers Company. In 1955, the company opened an automated biscuit factory near Liverpool, and the Reading workforce waited with some trepidation for automation to hit them, but in 1977 the Reading factory was closed entirely, ending 150 years of biscuit making in the town.

The Palmer family's charitable contributions to Reading ought not to be forgotten. The most obvious is the park in east Reading that bears the family name and was donated to the town by them, but they also helped to fund what would become Reading University, paid for part of Reading's first library and gave the town 12 acres of recreational space at King's Meadow, among other charitable donations.

Whilst Huntley & Palmers are the biscuit maker everyone remembers, let it not be forgotten that Reading had a second manufacturer. Serpell's started life in 1851 in Plymouth, making ships' biscuits (the kind sailors traditionally had to bang on the table before eating, to make the weevils fall out). They diversified into fancy biscuits, but in 1869 their premises were destroyed by fire and rebuilt. They outgrew the new factory, and in 1899 relocated to premises in South Street, Reading. These in turn caught fire in July 1904 and were rebuilt within eight weeks. They co-existed in a friendly way with Huntley & Palmers, even doing some sub-contracting for them in the 1950s, before the company went into liquidation in 1959.

BULBS: SUTTONS SEEDS

Suttons Seeds (and bulbs) were the third of Reading's staple Victorian industries. John Sutton set up a corn and seed merchant's business in Reading in 1807, but it was his son, Martin Hope Sutton, who built it into a major concern. In 1828, at the tender age of 13, he started trading as a seed merchant on his own account. In the 1830s he opened a seed trial ground, and he became a partner in his father's business at the age of 21.

The firm became the Royal Seed Establishment after it developed a business relationship with the bailiff of the Royal Home Farm at Windsor, and the government sought their help in dealing with the Irish potato famine of 1845. They were able to supply alternative crops and prevent a desperate situation from becoming even worse.

Two factors aided the growth of their business. One was their honest dealing. Adulteration of seed was commonplace at the time, and their scrupulousness made them stand out. The other was the introduction of the penny post, which enabled them to use mail order to grow from a local to a national business.

Their original premises were on the east side of the Market Place, but by the 1920s they had grown enormously to cover much of the area between King's Road, Abbey Street, the Forbury and Market Place. In addition, they had large trial grounds next to the railway on the edge of town.

The family were also active in the life of the town. Martin John Sutton stood as the town's mayor, and another family member, Herbert, helped in 1893 to found the University Extension College, which would grow into Reading University. They finally left the town in 1974, for Torquay, taking advantage of the high price they could get for their landholdings in Reading (the Suttons Industrial Park now stands on the site of their trial grounds).

CAR INDUSTRY

Believe it or not, Berkshire has, at various times, had its own car industry – some of it quite small and stuttering, but one part of it of major importance.

Taking the earliest – and quite probably the least – first, the British Motor and Engineering Company had a shadowy existence between 1905 and 1907. All we know is that they produced four models and were based in Caversham, Reading. Caversham Road was also the location of the Warwick Motor Carrier Company, one of three Berkshire motor car manufacturers listed in the 1915 *Kelly's Directory*. If their advertisements are to be believed, they were suppliers of motorised delivery vehicles to such prestigious companies as Harrods and Selfridges.

Herbert Engineering were positively glittering by comparison. During the First World War they made a living repairing broken fighter aircraft engines. When the demand for this understandably declined at the end of the war, they turned their attention to motor cars. Between 1919 and 1931 they turned out some 2,500 cars. These were quality products, designed to rival the likes of Bentley, and set speed records at Brooklands. Their earliest models would do 65+mph and their 1929 model was capable of 75–80mph. They were victims of the depression, however, and their premises were taken over by Thorneycroft.

Post-war, Reading resident Derek Buckler set up his own car manufacturers in Crowthorne. Between 1947 and 1962 (when he retired on health grounds) they produced some 500 cars, starting with the Mark V (and before you ask, there were no Marks I to IV – he just did not want people thinking they were getting an untested prototype). Although the engines in them were sometimes feeble (in at least one case an 1,172cc engine from a clapped-out Ford van), they had an advanced space frame design, and one of them won a national economy run, achieving 91mpg over a 600-mile course.

His other claim to fame (according to Buckler enthusiasts) was as a talented tax avoider. He is credited with helping to start the kit car industry as a means of avoiding the crippling post-war purchase tax on complete new vehicles. It is even claimed that he persuaded the taxman that his cars were left-hand drive (and thus intended for export and tax exempt), by reversing the negative of the photographs of the cars when he printed them! He also made components for other manufacturers, including Lotus, and built an early chassis for the Brabham racing team. He went into racing kart manufacturing, and his employee, Jack Barlow, produced his Barlotti karts until 1990. In 1997, twelve surviving Bucklers were driven in a motorcade through Reading to mark their jubilee.

Slough has had quite a diverse involvement with the motor industry. The sleek Peerless sports coupe was built in Slough between 1957 and 1960. It used Triumph TR3 components and about 325 were built, including one that took sixteenth place at the Le Mans twenty-four hour race in 1958. The model was rejuvenated as the Warwick, which was built in Colnbrook between 1960 and 1962. Some versions of this used big American engines, and the car later evolved into the Gordon Keeble. Sleeker still was the Ford GT40, a three times Le Mans winner developed at Slough, as was the McLaren M6, a road-going version of their racer. This was developed on the Poyle Trading Estate, Colnbrook in 1969. Lola drove their Mark 6 GT car direct from their Slough factory to France, to take part in the 1963 Le Mans race.

Citroën assembled cars in Slough between 1925 and 1966, at a factory later used by Mars. One of their more unusual offerings, from 1959–64, was the Bijou, essentially a 2CV with a heavy glass fibre body that made it even slower than the already sluggish 2CV. It was said to be capable of about 45mph 'on a good day' and a 0–40 time of 41.7 seconds (the more conventional 0–60 time was only obtainable by pushing it off a tall building). Only about 210 were ever sold.

Ford built lorries at its Langley plant from 1936 to the 1950s, and Honda have their UK head office (but no car manufacturing) at Slough.

By far the most important contribution Berkshire has made to the motor industry was from a factory in Abingdon (until 1974 part of Berkshire). In its day, more sports cars were made there than anywhere else in the world.

Cecil Kimber joined Morris Garages in 1921 as a sales manager. His contacts with the wealthy Oxford undergraduates (where Morris Garages were based) persuaded him that, if they could build a car that was 10 per cent better, they could charge 50 per cent more for it. To test his theory, he commissioned some custom-built bodies which he bolted onto the standard (and decidedly pedestrian) Morris Cowley chassis. When these proved difficult to shift at his inflated price, he went a stage further and started improving the running gear as well. This gave rise to the 1924 MG Special four-seat sports car, which was the first car to carry the distinctive MG badge. This led, in turn, to the first racing MG – the old Number 1 – which proved itself at the 1925 Land's End Trial, and started the sporting tradition that was an important part of the MG image. The MG marque became so successful that they soon outgrew their production space in Oxford and the parent Morris Garages Company funded their move in 1929 to new premises in Abingdon, into a former leather goods factory.

By the late 1920s there was a real need for economy motoring. The government was taxing cars on the basis of their 'treasury rating', essentially a measure of engine capacity, and petrol tax (scrapped in 1919) had been reintroduced, taking petrol costs to a crippling 18½d per gallon (in modern terms, about 1.7p per litre). This led Morris to produce the first Morris Minor, which they powered with a detuned version of an 847cc Wolseley engine. Kimber got hold of the non-detuned version of the engine, and put it in a small sports car with a plywood and fabric body. The first MG Midget was born, selling for £175, little more than a standard Morris Minor.

During the war car production ceased, and the works was turned over to making and servicing tanks, making munitions and other war work. After the war, the ruined state of the national economy meant they had to concentrate on the hitherto neglected export market, and in particular the United States. All they had to offer was the MGTC – essentially a development of the MGTA from 1936. Though it was increasingly outdated in looks and performance, the Americans took it to their hearts and from 1950 they were selling 10,000 cars a year, 90 per cent of them being exported (despite not even having a left-hand drive option).

In 1952 they tried to bring in a radically updated model, but it fell foul of boardroom politics. The parent Morris Company was, by now, part of the Nuffield Group, which had merged (inter alia) with Austin. They were in the process of launching their Austin Healey 100 sports car, and did not want a rival launching alongside it. So MG were forced to soldier on with further makeovers of their old models until 1955, when they could produce a proper 1950s sports car, the MGA. With styling based on their 1951 Le Mans racer, it was another great success, both at home and abroad, selling 20,571 in 1957 alone, and 17,195 of those for the American market.

It was followed, in the 1960s, by the MGB and its derivatives (including a 130mph V8 version, unhelpfully launched around the time of the 1973–75 petrol crisis) and a new version of the MG Midget. By now, production was up to 55,000 cars a year. But MG had never bothered to streamline their production methods throughout their time at Abingdon, and according to the accountants at the Leyland Group (of which they were now part) they were losing

£900 on every car they sold. In the face of passionate opposition from the workforce and MG enthusiasts the factory was closed in October 1980, after having produced over 1 million cars and given employment to up to 1,200 people. Only the brand lived on, with MG badges being used to add some spurious sporting credibility to the sometimes stodgy products of the parent company, until its own demise. Even the brand has since been sold to the Chinese.

14

NEW BERKSHIRE? SLOUGH AND BRACKNELL

In this chapter, we look at two parts of Berkshire that may be thought of as 'new'. Bracknell may be seen as the product of post-war new town planning, while Slough seems to be largely the result of twentieth-century industrial growth. Moreover, Slough is 'new' to Berkshire in the sense of only having joined it in 1974, but both these settlements have a lot more history to them than meets the eye.

SLOUGH

Contrary to popular belief, Slough is not a recent invention. Many of its suburbs – Upton, Chalvey, Cippenham and Langley – were Saxon, with over 1,000 years of settlement history. Slough itself made an appearance within a century of the Norman Conquest, albeit just as a crossroad on the London–Bristol route, where the road from Windsor Castle joined the main highway. The name 'Slough' means a muddy area and, although the town centre itself is on relatively high, dry ground, some surrounding areas like Chalvey were extremely boggy, and the road to Windsor could be almost impassable in winter.

When the construction of Eton College began in the 1440s, it was one of the first British buildings to use the new-fangled continental construction method – brick. Slough's clays proved ideal for making them and, over a period of about nine years, some 2,500,000 bricks were supplied to the college. It was the start of an industry that would continue into the nineteenth century.

By 1557, the settlement was important enough to boast three ale houses (though, to put it in context, Colnbrook had eight). Part of the main coaching route between London and Bath and Bristol ran down, what is now, Slough High Street. The first coach came through in 1657 and Slough gradually became established as a stopping place. The Colnbrook Turnpike Trust was established in 1718 to improve the maintenance of the coach road, though they were not spectacularly successful in doing so.

By the eighteenth century, Slough had grown to about thirty houses – seven of them ale houses – but Salt Hill, a small settlement about 1 mile to the west, was now competing for their coach trade. Daniel Defoe, passing through the town in the early eighteenth century, observed that Slough seemed to consist almost entirely of inns. 'They seem to vie with one another, and 'tis wonderful how they all subsist.'

It was in 1786 that the village received a distinguished new resident. William Herschel was the astronomer who discovered the planet Uranus. He had been appointed personal astronomer to King George III, and came to live in Slough to be within easy access of Windsor. Herschel put Slough on the map – literally – for the massive 40ft telescope he erected on his premises was shown as a separate feature on the first Ordnance Survey map of the area.

By 1816, Slough and Upton could, together, boast a population of 500, and its 1823 *Trade Directory* was bursting with no less than twenty-one businesses. The coach business was booming, with almost fifty coaches a day coming through the town by 1836, heading to or from a variety of destinations – Birmingham, Oxford, Worcester and Gloucester, as well as Bristol and Bath. But they were in for a major shake-up, as the Great Western Railway advanced westwards out of London to steal their long-distance trade. By June 1838, it had reached its initial terminus near Maidenhead. Slough's initial difficulty in securing a station of its own is detailed in the transport chapter but, with or without a proper station, the railway marked the start of a major period of growth for the town.

In the 1851 Census Slough had a population of over 1,500, and 103 shops and businesses. There was even public sector job growth, as the Union Workhouse for southern Buckinghamshire had chosen to locate near to Slough. The railway built a palatial new hotel, the Royal, near the station. It had a private waiting room for Queen Victoria to use when going to or from Windsor. However, this was one venture that was doomed as soon as the Windsor branch line was opened in 1849, and the hotel closed four years later.

By this time, Slough's brickworks were selling much of their production in London. Once the canal was opened, barges laden with bricks would head off down the Grand Union Canal and would return loaded with London's refuse and other waste. Some of this waste material was used to landfill the worked-out brick fields or fertilise the town's crops, but that part which could be burned was used to fire the brick kilns. This cheap fuel helped Slough bricks to compete when the automation of brickworks in Bedfordshire was giving them a competitive advantage in other respects.

The dust and smoke of the brickworks, along with the landfill being dumped, cannot have made Slough the most desirable of residential environments, so it may be surprising that one of its other successful nineteenth-century industries was agriculture. Slough was the home of various varieties of apple, the most famous being Cox's Orange Pippin, first grown in Cippenham in 1825. Another variety – Mrs Simpkin's Pink – was named after the matron of the local workhouse in the 1880s.

Another smell which may have competed for the residents' attention was embrocation. James Elliman Senior founded his business in Slough in about 1847. His son built an embrocation factory in Chandos Street and, among other gifts to the town, gave them the Salt Hill Playing Fields.

During the First World War, plans were put in train to create a mechanical transport repair depot at Cippenham Court Farm, but the war ended before it could be completed. The government was left with a 600-acre area, covered in scrap machinery – a white elephant and an embarrassment to them, known locally as 'the Dump'. It was

with some relief that they let a consortium of businessmen take it off their hands. Having made a considerable profit from the sale of the scrap by 1925, the consortium changed its name to Slough Estates and set about developing the Slough Trading Estate. Over the years, it has housed the production of a host of consumer products – from Citroën cars, Gillette razors, Black & Decker tools, Mars bars (at their peak, producing 3 million a day), to the *Thunderbirds* television puppet series and a real life thunderbird, the Ford GT40 sports car.

It was a great success. During the lean times of the 1920s and 1930s, Slough had an unemployment rate of just 1 per cent, and they had to promote a major house building programme in response to the influx of jobseekers from Wales and the north. The *Daily Mail* called Slough 'the hardest working town in Britain', where overtime rather than short time was the norm, and neither house- nor factory-building could keep up with demand. Not everybody felt so warmly about the place; it was the trading estate that prompted John Betjeman's famous poem 'Slough' in 1937, from which civic pride has been smarting ever since. The Trading Estate only became administratively part of Slough in 1930/31, when the town's boundaries were adjusted to fit with the new reality.

What is needed is a touch of romance to relieve Slough's somewhat workaday image. How about the fact that Richard, Earl of Cornwall, the son of King John, spent his honeymoon in Cippenham, following his marriage in the year 1231? However, I have struggled to find any royals, or indeed other notables, who have subsequently followed his example.

BRACKNELL – THE ANCIENT NEW TOWN

The casual visitor to the centre of Bracknell might be forgiven for thinking that it had no history before the New Towns Act of 1946, but they would be very wrong.

People have been living in the area for more than 2,000 years. Caesar's Camp (the earthworks were mistakenly attributed to Julius of that ilk) is an Iron Age hill fort, put there by Celts, possibly as early as 300 BC. An early version of its name – 'braccan heal' (other spellings are available) – appears in a Saxon charter of AD 942. It means 'a spur of land covered with bracken' (or possibly a spur of land belonging to someone called Bracca).

Easthamstead sort of appears in Domesday Book, except that the clerks making the record seem to have misheard what the locals said its name was, and wrote it down as 'Lachenestede' (it should have been 'Yethampstede'). This means 'the homestead by the gate', the gate in question being a gap in the fence to allow the king's deer to pass in and out. This tells us that the area formed part of the Royal Forest at Windsor, used by successive monarchs for hunting.

Until the untimely end of Charles I's reign, there were very strict rules about what anyone living in a royal forest (or the heathland that adjoined it) could or could not do. For example, the royal deer were protected, and hence multiplied to a point where they left no food in the forest for any other creature. So hard did the rules make life for residents that many law abiding citizens preferred to live just outside it, leaving the forest itself to those of a more criminal disposition. Many a highwayman practiced his trade in the woods and a 1692 Act offered a £40 reward for bringing any one of them to justice.

By 1847, *Kelly's Directory* said of Bracknell that the village itself consists of 'a long narrow street, inhabited principally by small shopkeepers'. But the village was beginning to grow. It got its own church in 1851, and a railway linking it to Reading and London (Waterloo) followed in 1856. Among other things, this made it easier to import coal, and gave a major boost to the local brick making industry, which soon became the area's largest employer. Between 1841 and 1871 the village roughly doubled in size, from 2,000 to 4,000, but it was still only a small town of about 6,000 by the 1940s.

It was the Greater London Plan of 1944 that first floated the idea of a ring of ten satellite towns, outside the new London Green Belt, to ease housing pressures in the capital. At first they proposed a new settlement of 60,000 people at White Waltham, but the idea was eventually rejected because it would take too much good quality farmland and because there would be conflict between a new town and a working airfield (White Waltham Airfield was being intensively used during the war years). Various alternatives were considered – Didcot, Goring, Thame, Frimley, Thatcham and Romsey, but by June 1947 they settled on a much smaller new settlement of 25,000 people at Bracknell.

Objections to the original 1948 Designation Order led to the exclusion of 773 acres from the original site, and the 25,000 growth limit soon proved to be unrealistic. It was virtually exceeded by the early 1960s. By 1957 the target was raised to 40,000 and by 1962 to 61,000. Meanwhile, the first house was handed over to its tenant on 11 October 1951, and construction of a new town centre began in 1955. By 1961, the population of Bracknell had already reached 20,533 and by 1973 it was up to 45,000. The Development Corporation was finally wound up in June 1982.

Those who fret about the length of time modern day planning processes take might want to reflect on the timetable followed by the 1940s Minister of Town Planning, Lewis Silkin. Although his civil servants had been working on the new town plans for ages, once they got into the public realm everything went forward at a blistering speed. It was initially proposed to hold the public inquiry into the new town on 21 January 1949, just two weeks after the closing date for objections to it. Public opinion forced him to put it back, at least to early February but, even so, the inquiry was completed and the inspector's report written and in the minister's hands by early March.

Silkin's attitude to consultation can be judged by what happened in the parallel process at the Stevenage New Town site. Confronted by a storm of protest at a public meeting, Silkin shouted at them 'It's no good your jeering! It's going to be done!' Small wonder satirical protesters changed the name plates at Stevenage railway station to 'Silkingrad'. When he came to Bracknell, protesters shouted 'Gestapo!' and 'Dictator!' at him, and put sand in the ministerial car's petrol tank.

The new town was predictably unpopular with local residents, who did not take to the idea of hordes of Londoners moving in. It was even less popular when people learned that it was intended to be exclusively for Londoners – Berkshire people need not apply for houses. As John Rowley, the one-time general manager of the new town put it, 'We are about as popular as rattlesnakes with the old Bracknellians.' And in case you think Prince Charles was the first royal to try and influence planning decisions, the Queen was said to have offered her own cutting edge urban design advice to the New Town's chairman, Sir Lancelot Keay, telling him: 'I hear you are building a town on our doorstep. Make it look nice, now.'

It was said that this comment was one of the factors that led the designers to favour low-rise housing over high-rise flats, and conventional materials and design over modern alternatives. One thing they, like most planners of the day, got very wrong was accommodating the motor car. When, in 1951, the Corporation submitted plans for 121 houses with forty-seven garages, the Ministry told them the number of garages was excessive. Fourteen per 100 houses would be quite enough, and even by 1971, they did not expect the need to exceed twenty-one per 100 houses. Predictably, a huge waiting list for garages sprang up – by 1952, demand was already exceeding 1971 forecasts and by 1962, over half the residents had, or had their names down for, a garage.

The intention was that it would not be just a housing estate but a self-contained community, with a balance between jobs and housing, and with all the necessary community facilities in place. Proposals to build new factories earned the scheme a new opponent in the form of the Federation of British Industries, who objected on the grounds that there was already a labour shortage in the area.

There was no shortage of firms interested in moving to Bracknell, but it was not easily done. In those days you needed an Industrial Development Certificate, and it was the government's priority to get firms to move to the more benighted parts of the kingdom, not leafy Berkshire. Local firms, already experiencing labour shortages, even lobbied the BBC to promote their campaign for more house building. When one high tech manufacturer heard that the cameras were coming, he sent all his workers home so that the cameras would show only untended machines that should have been earning foreign exchange. Oddly, it took about ten years for the Development Corporation to hit on the idea of attracting white collar, as opposed to industrial, jobs. The Meteorological Office were the first big office employer to move into the town, in 1960–62.

The town did attract a variety of employers. To take just one of these, Racal was started in Isleworth in 1950 by Raymond Brown and Calder Cunningham (hence RA-CAL), both of whom put £50 into the new company. They came to Bracknell in 1954, no doubt attracted by the ninety-nine year lease on their new factory at 4s 6d (22p) a square foot, and no rent reviews. And were they successful? Just a bit. One of the many sidelines they gave birth to was a little company called 'Vodafone', and £1,000 invested in Racal in 1961 would have been worth £14.5 million by the year 2000.

15

AND ANOTHER THING …

This section gives us an opportunity to bring together stories about Berkshire that did not fit neatly into any of the other chapters.

THE BERKSHIRE LADY

Frances Kendrick was a spirited young woman of 17. She was independently wealthy, having inherited the Calcot Park estate, near Reading, on the death of her parents. She attended a wedding in 1707, at which she met an impoverished young attorney called Benjamin Child, who was apparently 'remarkably handsome' with 'sweet behaviour and courteous carriage'. She fell instantly in love with him, but he did not show any interest in her, despite her having (according to the same records) 'a great store of wealth and beauty' and 'a noble disposition'. Possibly he felt himself too much her social inferior, or assumed that such a catch as her would already be spoken for.

Frances hit upon an unusual way of getting his undivided attention. She sent him an anonymous challenge to a duel, allegedly arising from some offence he had caused. Benjamin turned up at the appointed time and place, no doubt puzzled as to who he had offended and how. He was none too pleased to find that his would-be opponent was a woman and, moreover, one who came in disguise. When he appeared unwilling to fight her, she offered him a choice – fight me or marry me. But if you marry me, you will not see my face until after we are wed.

Child opted for the really dangerous option; he put away his sword and agreed to marry her. He was swiftly whisked off to St Mary's Church, Reading, where the pre-arranged ceremony took place. Afterwards she took him back to her luxurious home and removed her disguise, and Child found he had hit the jackpot – a bride that was both beautiful, rich and sweet-natured. The marriage was predictably a very happy one, producing three daughters. The sad ending was that Frances only lived to be 35, and that Benjamin never really recovered from her loss.

This romantic episode, which is believed to be historically accurate, was captured in the ballad 'The Berkshire Lady'.

VIRGINIA WATER

Strictly speaking, Virginia Water lies within Runnymede District and is thus currently part of Surrey, but it is also part of Windsor Great Park, which is good enough for our purposes. The lake was originally little more than a stream, until William Duke of Cumberland and Ranger of the Royal Park developed plans for it.

Accounts differ as to precisely who dug the lake – some say it was Jacobite prisoners of war, others that it was English troops, stood down after the Battle of Culloden, or Hanoverian mercenaries that did the work. Whoever it was, by 1752 there was a large artificial lake in place. The work was not done well enough, however, because in 1768 a storm broke down the dam that contained it, with the loss of several lives.

William died in 1765, but it was not until 1780 that Paul and Thomas Sandby began building the much larger lake that we see today. They added the artificial waterfall and the Obelisk Pond. The Roman ruins of Leptis Magna were a later addition still, imported from Libya in 1818. It is today the largest ornamental artificial lake in England. It was drained during the Second World War, so as not to provide a useful navigation aid to German bombers, looking for Windsor. Its most recent claim to fame has been as the backdrop to lakeland scenes in the *Harry Potter* films. And in case you are wondering where the water comes from, Virginia Water is fed by the River Bourne, which makes its exit after tumbling down the waterfall.

EARLY MOTORING AND THE PROTEST MOTORIST

Berkshire was witness to almost the first (some wrongly claim it was the very first) motor car journey to be made in Britain, and it was carried out with the express intention of attracting a prosecution. In 1895, motor cars in Britain were subject to absurdly restrictive legislation (including a 4mph speed limit), that stifled both their use and the development of a home grown car industry. In that year, the Honourable Evelyn Ellis brought the Panhard-Levassor car that he had used on the Continent back to England. It was delivered by train to Micheldever in Hampshire, and Ellis then drove it back to his home in Datchet, at a highly illegal 10mph and without a man walking in front, as the law also required. On the 56-mile journey they reported passing 133 horses, only two of which showed any agitation at their passing.

The event received wide press coverage, but the police were disappointingly unwilling to give Ellis his day in court to expose the absurdity of the laws (which were in any case repealed the following year). The *Windsor and Eton Express* was among the newspapers that covered the story in detail, and one of the things their readers wanted to know was whether the vehicle was easy to drive. 'Not by a lady', they concluded, for 'a firm grip of the steering handle and a keen eye are necessary'.

In 1896, Ellis gave the future King Edward VII his first drive in a motor car, starting the monarch's lifelong interest in them. There are further postscripts to this story: one of Ellis' neighbours, who owned Ditton Park, Datchet, was John Douglas-Scott-Montagu, who went on to found the National Motor Museum at Beaulieu. As for Ellis' car, it can now been seen in the Science Museum; and Ellis' daughter, Mary, went on to race cars at Brooklands and met her future husband after his horse shied upon encountering her motor vehicle.

By 1900, motorists were liberated, allowed to speed along at a dizzying 12mph, and the people of Berkshire saw probably the biggest parade of horseless carriages that any of them had ever witnessed. On 23 April, some sixty-five cars set out from London on a 1,000-mile trial run around Britain, designed to show that the motor car was a practical proposition. Their route brought them through Reading, and down the A4 en route to Bristol, stopping on the way at Calcot Park, where they were entertained by the race's sponsor, the newspaper magnate Alfred Harmsworth (later Lord Northcliffe). According to contemporary press reports:

> The motorists were all covered in dust and were for the most clad in thick coats, with peaked caps and a pair of uncoloured glass goggles with leather dustproof flaps, which gave them the appearance of an uncouth-looking highwayman of the olden days.

Just thirty-five of the sixty-five starters completed the course, but even this was taken to herald a great advance in the cause of motoring, showing that:

> ... The motor car is, even in its present state of development, a serious and trustworthy means of locomotion; not a toy, dangerous and troublesome alike to the public and its owner, but a vehicle under as perfect control as a Bath chair...

The year of 1904 saw the speed limit raised again, to 20mph, but a number of councils including Slough, Colnbrook and Reading petitioned for a limit of just 10mph in their built-up areas. Berkshire councillors railed against inconsiderate motorists and got their clerk to canvass other authorities, with a view to lobbying the home secretary for tighter controls over them. Early speed traps were set up in Bracknell High Street, but the councillors could only dream of sentences like that given to Berkshire's most famous fictitious motorist, Mr Toad of *The Wind in the Willows*, who got twenty years in gaol for his reckless driving.

Higher speeds also meant more dust. Eton Wick Council used a water cart to dampen the road in an effort to keep the dust down, but after an acrimonious correspondence in the local paper, Twyford Parish Council went for the radical step of tarring the local roads at a cost of £40.

SOME BERKSHIRE MARTYRS

Religion was a dangerous activity to be involved with in sixteenth-century Berkshire. In this section we encounter some who paid the ultimate price for their faith.

The Berkshire Lollards

Some of the earliest of Berkshire's heretics were the Lollards, followers of the theologian John Wycliffe (d.1384), who invited persecution by proposing the novel idea that Christians should be obedient to God and the Bible, rather than to the Church and its traditions (such as 'fast-tracking' rich men to heaven).

West Berkshire had a tradition of Lollard nonconformity dating back at least to 1450, and Jack Cade's Rebellion. In the course of this, William Ainscough, Bishop of Salisbury and a noted prosecutor of Lollards, was murdered. One of the rebels was in due course caught, tried, hanged and quartered. His mangled body (or part of it) was put on display at Newbury, as a warning to any like-minded nonconformists, there or in Hungerford, the other Berkshire hotbed of dissent.

Isolated cases were detected and dealt with on an ad hoc basis in the area until 1521, when John Longland was made Bishop of Lincoln. He promptly began a vigorous programme of hunting heretics down across several counties, including Berkshire. A single dissident (one Robert Pope) was 'persuaded' to condemn no less than eighty-seven local people (including his own father, wife and brother). Four of them were burnt at the stake and over fifty suffered lesser punishments, from deprivation of food to branding on the cheek.

The Last Abbot

Hugh Faringdon was born Hugh Cook, but took the name of his place of origin as his own. He entered the Church and rose to become the abbot of Reading Abbey in 1520 – a man of some influence in Tudor society. He was on good terms with Henry VIII, entertained him at the abbey and offered his help in brokering Henry's divorce from Catherine of Aragon. What he could not accept, however, was the idea of Henry as the head of the Church in England. In September 1539, Reading Abbey was formally dissolved and Faringdon was arrested and taken to the Tower of London. He was sent back to Reading 'to be tried and executed' (which cannot have left him with much optimism for the outcome of the trial). He was found guilty of high treason and was sentenced to death by hanging, drawing and quartering. On 14 November he was dragged through the streets of Reading to the Forbury, where the gibbet stood on the site now occupied by St James RC Church. There he was hanged with two colleagues and, according to the barbarous terms of his sentence, should have been taken down alive from it so that he could witness his own disembowelling. Mercifully, he was dead when they cut him down. He was made a saint by Pope Leo XIII in 1895.

The Windsor Protestants

By 1543 there was a Catholic backlash against the Protestant reforms introduced earlier in Henry VIII's reign. (For all the reforms carried out in his name, Henry himself was never a convinced Protestant, and the Six Articles, approved in 1539, reinforced a traditional view of the Church and the clergy.)

Henry Filmer, Robert Testwood and Anthony Pearson were all quite prominent Protestants in Windsor. All had managed in some way to offend William Simonds, a former mayor of Windsor, a Catholic and a man with the ear of some influential people. He pursued his grudge and managed to get the three of them tried for heresy, using the Six Articles. They were found guilty, after Simonds allegedly threatened the jury, and on 4 August 1543 the three Windsor martyrs were burned at the stake, roughly where the Riverside Station stands today. Simonds and others were later found guilty of a conspiracy in securing the convictions. Their much more modest sentence was to be pilloried, and to ride round the town on their horses, sitting back to front and wearing paper caps.

The Master of Reading School

By 1556 the swing back to Catholicism was in full flow under Catholic Queen Mary.

Julius (or Julins or Joscelyn) Palmer had started life as a Catholic, but while up at Oxford he witnessed the martyrdom of the Protestants Latimer and Ridley. Their steadfast faith (and the barbaric treatment they received) caused Palmer to change his own views. This, in turn, caused him to be labelled a heretic and he was driven out of Oxford.

He became Master of Reading School, but the heretic label followed him. He fled the school, but made the mistake of returning there to collect some of his possessions and back pay. He was betrayed and arrested, charged with sedition and religious heresy. Tried at Newbury on 16 July 1555, he was found guilty and immediately

Bishop Ridley

burnt at the stake with two others, John Gwyn and Thomas Robyns (or Askin). As they died, the three of them reportedly cried out: 'Lord Jesu strengthen us! Lord Jesu assist us! Lord Jesu receive our souls!' Palmer was just 24 years old when he died.

A much more pragmatic (if less principled) approach to religion was that adopted by Berkshire's 'Vicar of Bray', who changed his religious beliefs repeatedly to suit the orthodoxy of the day. The term has come to mean anyone who bends with the wind in an unprincipled way. Exactly which Vicar of Bray this relates to is not clear, since the term can apply to two periods of religious turbulence – 1533–59 (Henry VIII–Elizabeth I) and 1633–1715 (Charles I–George I).

In the earlier period there was a vicar of Bray, Simon Aleyn, who changed religion five times. Among the candidates for the latter period was the vicar, Simon Simonds, who adopted four different creeds. Whoever he was, the vicar rebutted the charge of inconsistency. He told accusers: 'I have always kept my principle, which is this, to live and die the Vicar of Bray'. The character prompted a satirical song, an 1882 comic opera and a 1937 film starring Stanley Holloway.

SLAVERY AND GENTRY

Slavery was widespread in Norman England. According to Domesday Book, 13 per cent of Berkshire's population were slaves. Of the rest, 31 per cent were bordars, 11 per cent cottars and 44 per cent villeins, all of whom were to varying degrees in a state of serfdom – subject to a lord and required to carry out labour services for him. Only a tiny proportion of the population could claim to be fully free men.

As for the size of the population, 6,160 people were actually mentioned in Berkshire's part of Domesday Book. They were probably household heads, so multiply them by the average household size of the day – estimated at between three and a half and five – to give a total figure for Berkshire of between 21,560 and 30,800 (there are uncertainties as to how slaves were recorded, but let's not get into details).

By contrast, Berkshire was, by 1665, awash with nobility. A survey that year recorded some 900 families (representing around 6 per cent of the county's population of around 71,000) as being 'gentry'. This compares with a national average of around 3–4 per cent. But, of these, only five families were members of the peerage, a further fourteen were baronets, thirteen knights and eighty to ninety esquires – the remainder were mere common or garden gentry.

FEEDING THE POOR

Speenhamland, near Newbury, was the setting for an important revision to the welfare arrangements for the needy. It looked to give additional aid to the industrious poor, who were suffering dreadfully by 1795. They linked the payment of relief to the price of bread and the size of the individual's family. The well-intentioned Speenhamland system soon became very unpopular, since it encouraged farmers to underpay their workers, in the knowledge that they would have any shortfall made up by the parish. This upset both the workers, who did not like being dependent on charity, and those who had to fund the additional burden on poor relief.

The workhouse was an ever-present threat for Berkshire's poor. Berkshire had forty-five of them by the beginning of the nineteenth century, and some (Abingdon, Newbury and Reading) had been in existence since before the Civil War. They were mostly small establishments, and were concentrated into twelve larger Poor Law Unions, with a harsh regime to discourage all but the most desperate, following national legislation in 1834. Care was supposed to be

given only to inmates of the workhouse, where husbands, wives, children, the able-bodied and infirm were all to be separated from each other. As the Poor Law Commissioners caringly put it:

> Every penny bestowed that tends to render the condition of the pauper more eligible than that of the independent labourer, is a bounty on indolence and vice.

The local Poor Law Unions did not always see eye to eye with their national masters. Wokingham, for example, challenged the principle of separating the elderly into male and female wards, and Newbury introduced a dietary plan more generous than the national guidelines allowed. These Victorian institutions remained responsible for poor relief until 1930, when the local authorities took over.

TWO SIDES TO VICTORIAN READING

Reading was a town of contrasts. On the one hand, the Boundary Commission said that it was 'a place of considerable size, population and apparent prosperity ... The main streets are spacious, and contain very good shops and are well-lighted by gas.' On the other, a correspondent to the local newspaper in 1846 complained that no one could pass down a side street without being offended 'by some stagnant pool of putridity, the insufferable stench of a slaughter-house, or the foul air of a half-choked drain'. Even the main streets were said to be almost unendurable in hot weather. There were pigsties and slaughter houses in full view of passers-by, and heaps of foul untended refuse in the streets. One reformer called Reading 'nothing but an extended cesspool'. Small wonder that the town had the highest mortality rate in Berkshire.

Legislation in 1848 allowed local authorities to set up Boards of Health to tackle these problems, and Reading's was established in 1850. For decades there would be a running battle between the reformers and the so-called 'economisers', like one Alderman Brown, who jibbed at the cost, and argued in 1859 that the prevention of fever was impious and that to suggest that a good drainage system would prevent disease was saying more than mortal man ought to do. It took until 1875 to get a decent sewerage system in the town, and 1878 to get a reliable, clean water supply.

FASCINATING FACTS

Do you feel inadequate? Do you fail to dazzle people with your conversation? That is probably because you did not know the following facts about Berkshire, with which to delight and amaze your friends and family. In no order whatsoever:

Wokingham's first royal charter, granted by Elizabeth I, allowed the authorities to appoint two constables – and two ale tasters. The town (as it now is) was founded by a thirteenth-century Norman-French bishop, named Roger le Poore.

London has Big Ben (the largest bell in Parliament's clock tower) but Reading has 'Harry', a great bell in the tower of St Lawrence's Church, donated in 1493 by a wealthy clothier named Henry Kelsall.

Two Berkshire MPs, Henry Martin of Coley and Daniel Blagrave of Reading, were signatories to the death warrant of King Charles I.

The Swan public house in Pangbourne used to sit right on the border of Oxfordshire and Berkshire – in fact the boundary line went right through the two bars. The licensing laws differed between the two counties, with closing time half an hour later on one side than the other. Those wanting more drinking time simply carried their glasses to the appropriate part of the pub.

Queen Elizabeth I

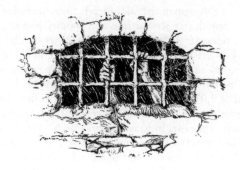

Eighteenth-century Berkshire had two county towns – the County Courts met at both Abingdon and Reading. The County Gaol was at Reading, but both towns had a 'Bridewell' (or house of correction). Abingdon was formally recognised as 'the Capital town of Berkshire' in its first charter, granted in 1556, and continued to be so until Reading took over in the 1860s. By then, Reading had long since surpassed Abingdon in size and importance.

The County Gaol was at Windsor between 1277 and 1314, at which time people complained to the king that Windsor was too small and remote to feed the prisoners properly, 'whereby the prisoners die immediately, as well the innocent as the guilty'. Windsor's gaol was demolished as a result of the coming of the railway in 1848. Also demolished was the adjoining George Street area – 'a scene of much squalor and depravity'. Wallingford Castle also contained a gaol.

What links Marlow with Hungary? Marlow Bridge, opened in 1832, so impressed a visiting Hungarian nobleman that he commissioned its designer, William Tierney Clark, to build a larger version of it across the River Danube, linking the towns of Buda and Pest.

A new dynasty was begun in Newbury on St Luke's Day 1483, when the Earl of Richmond was proclaimed king by Sir William Norris and Sir Thomas de la Mare. He would in 1485 officially become Henry VII, the first Tudor monarch. In 1688, William of Orange accepted the English throne at the Bear Hotel in Hungerford. Regime change was also afoot in 1400 at Windsor Castle. Richard II had been deposed the year before by Henry Bolingbroke (who became Henry IV). Supporters of Richard planned to infiltrate Windsor Castle during the 'Twelfth Night' festivities, and murder Henry and his four sons. But the plot was discovered and the plotters fled, some of them fighting a rearguard action against their pursuers at Maidenhead Bridge.

In 1517 a tithingman (parish official) from Braywick threatened one Alice Smythgate with a fine and 'bodily punishment' if she refused to refrain from 'babbling' and 'using her unruly tongue'.

On 12 July 1901 Maidenhead experienced 92mm (3.6in) of rain in a single hour – the highest one hour of rainfall ever recorded in the United Kingdom. That record still stood in April 2011.

A total of 8,070 council houses were built in Berkshire between the two world wars. Almost 39 per cent of these (3,140) were built by Reading. The rents in some of Berkshire's rural districts had to be set at below national government guidelines, to take account of the very low agricultural wages in the area. Only 452 of Reading's council houses came with an electricity supply before the war. Some of those in rural areas of Berkshire did not even have running water or mains sewerage, relying on wells or boreholes, septic tanks or cesspools (and, of course, no bathrooms).

Until the twentieth century there was a toll for crossing Windsor Bridge. It cost the living 2*d*, but if you were dead the price went up to 6*s* 8*d* (33p)!

Christianity was brought to the Thames Valley by St Birinus (*c.* AD 600–649), who was born in modern-day Germany and landed at Hamwic (now Southampton) in AD 634. Sent there by the Pope, he began converting the people of Wessex, and was given the Bishopric of Dorchester, then the capital of Wessex. There are claims (though how solidly based it is difficult to tell) that he created the foundations for St Mary's Church in Reading, St Helens in Abingdon, and churches at Ipsden, Checkendon and Taplow, among others.

Some of the first hospitals in Berkshire were for lepers. Reading got one in the 1130s, Windsor in 1168 and Newbury and Hungerford got theirs sometime in the 1200s. Most of them closed in the fourteenth century, as the disease died out.

You might not think of Newbury as a focal point for the lifeboat industry but, for many years after 1816, the model designed by Newbury agricultural engineer, William Plenty, became the standard for lifeboat services all around our coasts.

Berkshire County Council took up its newly granted powers in 1889. Its income from the rates in the first year was just £11,944.

The day of 30 March 1851 saw the only census of the nation's religious practices. In Berkshire, the county's religious institutions had a capacity of 92,737 seats for a population of 170,065, 61 per cent of which were Church of England. Most of them offered two services on a Sunday and, ever since 1851, there have been

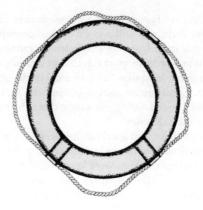

disputes about how to deal with double counting (since no names, just total attendances, were recorded).

Overall, Berkshire came out more religious than the national average (though neighbours Wiltshire and Buckinghamshire out-worshipped Berkshire) and west Berkshire proved to be more devout than the east. The Anglicans' share of the turnout was almost identical to their share of the seating, at 60.8 per cent.

Local areas noted for dissent since the seventeenth century, or even back into mediaeval times, continued to show up as hotbeds of nonconformity in the nineteenth century. Rural Berkshire in particular had a strong showing of Methodism, but Catholics were generally thin on the ground. Just 1,177 Catholic attendances were recorded, less than 2 per cent of the population, many of these either clustered around the homes of long-established Catholic gentry or in the main urban areas.

The present Wargrave Church replaces one that was destroyed by fire on Whit Sunday, 1914. It was burnt down by militant suffragettes. A service was held in the ruins of the church the following Sunday and, when the vicar denounced such militancy, a female member of the congregation shouted 'God bless Mrs Pankhurst' and was escorted out. Some say the perpetrators were angry because the vicar would not delete the word 'obey' from the marriage service, others that it was a protest against the forced feeding of their comrades in prison. St Mary's in Reading was also threatened with an attack, though it never materialised.

At the start of the nineteenth century, Berkshire had a population of 110,752, only about 3,000 of which were eligible to vote. There were no true 'pocket boroughs', where one person controlled who got elected, but there was still a good deal of corruption. In 1780 some £2,600 was spent from the king's private purse to 'encourage' the voters of Windsor to support the Crown's candidate, and many a rich candidate made similar 'investments' in the other Berkshire constituencies. Someone estimated around the same time that it would cost you about £4,000, excluding direct bribes, to secure a parliamentary seat in Reading.

Any gourmet in search of local cuisine need look no further than the Wokingham market of the eighteenth century. This specialised in fatted fowls, in which chickens were kept in darkness for a fortnight and forcibly fed with a diet of barley meal, suet and treacle. Those birds that did not die of this gastronomic nightmare were then sold for the table.

Forget Bath; Berkshire used to have its own spa – Sunninghill Wells. This became popular for the alleged curative properties of its water from the 1680s. Those who have sampled the water say it was yellow in colour and tasted of iron and sulphur. Leading figures in society apparently swore by its curative effects for gout, rheumatism and other ailments. However, it had apparently gone downmarket by the 1780s and was attracting a lower class of invalids.

Berkshire's first newspaper was the *Reading Mercury*, first published in 1723. It had only four pages and contained little or no local news. Others would follow – including the *Windsor and Eton Express* (1812), the *Berkshire Chronicle* (1825) and the *Slough Observer* (1883).

BERKSHIRE: THE PLACE TO BE

And finally, a note of triumph. In 2013, in a nationwide survey of towns and cities with a population of over 250,000 in Great Britain, Reading and Bracknell came out as the best places in the country in which to live. The criteria they used included the quality of transport, work/life balance, inequality, health, income levels, house prices relative to incomes, and the labour market. The next highest English town was Southampton, which could only manage fourth, with Cambridge and Oxford fifth and sixth. Quiet satisfaction may be had from the fact that London came close to bottom, along with Liverpool, Middlesbrough and Birmingham.

ABOUT THE AUTHOR

STUART HYLTON is the author of twenty regional and national books, including *Reading: The 1950s*, *Reading Then & Now*, *The Little Book of the 1950s* and *The Little Book of the 1970s*. He was born in Windsor and now lives in Reading, Berkshire.

If you enjoyed this book, you may also be interested in…

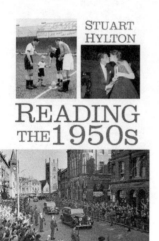

Reading: The 1950s
STUART HYLTON

From televisions to motor cars, this was a decade of rapid change for Reading. However, aspects also stayed much the same – the courage and humour of the townspeople in sometimes trying circumstances, the ingenuity and incompetence of the criminal classes and the sheer diversity of local life as it emerges from reports in the press. Capturing the spirit of the population during an era of bewildering development and change, this is a must-have for locals and anybody with an interest in the history of the town.

978 0 7524 9353 4

Thatcham Then & Now
NICK YOUNG

Contrasting a selection of forty-five archive images alongside full-colour modern photographs, this book looks at the historic Berkshire town of Thatcham during the last century. These intriguing photographs reveal changing modes of fashion and transportation, shops and businesses, houses and public buildings, and, of course, some of the local people who once lived and worked in the area. *Thatcham Then & Now* will awaken nostalgic memories for all who know this Berkshire town.

978 0 7524 6276 9